STORIES FROM THE
LAND OF ISRAEL

Rabbi Chanan Morrison

Stories from the Land of Israel

Copyright © 2015 Chanan Morrison

Second Edition.

ISBN: 1505499119
ISBN-13: 978-1505499117

Cover photo © Blitzkoenig, "Jaffa, Israel" (Dreamstime.com)

This book is dedicated to my grandchildren:

May they follow in the path of Israel's
illustrious scholars and *tzaddikim*
with a genuine love for
the People of Israel, the Land of Israel,
the Torah of Israel, and the God of Israel.

Contents

Jerusalem, 1919-1935

Rabbi Tzvi Yehudah Kook – Jerusalem

Rabbi Abraham Isaac HaKohen Kook (1865-1935)

Preface

Ordinarily, there are two dates inscribed on a tombstone: the deceased's date of birth and date of death. But should you visit Rabbi Abraham Isaac HaKohen Kook's grave in Jerusalem's ancient Mount of Olives cemetery – still in use after 3,000 years – you will find *three* dates engraved on his tombstone. Surprisingly, the first date inscribed there, the 28th of Iyyar, 5664 (the 13th of May, 1904), doesn't even refer to Rav Kook's birth.

And yet, this was a deeply significant date in Rav Kook's life. On this day – the same day on which the city of Jerusalem would be reunited 63 years later – a steamship sailing from Odessa docked at the port of Jaffa, bearing Rav Kook and his family.

At thirty-eight years old, Rav Kook was fulfilling a life-long aspiration and ascending to the Land of Israel. It was also a significant date for the Jewish people, marking the start of his remarkable career as philosopher and Kabbalist, public leader and Halakhic authority for the Jewish community in *Eretz Yisrael* and around the world – a profound influence that is still keenly felt a century later, as his writings are widely taught and studied.

The second date on Rav Kook's tombstone, the third of Elul, 5679, records a second "ascent," when he took up residence in the holy city of Jerusalem in the year 1919. And the third date – also the third of Elul – marks his final spiritual ascent, his passing on to the next world in 1935.

v

This book is not a biography. It is a selection of vignettes describing incidents in the lives of two spiritual giants: **Rabbi Abraham Isaac HaKohen Kook** (1865-1935), the celebrated first Chief Rabbi of pre-state Israel, and his son and spiritual successor, **Rabbi Tzvi Yehudah HaKohen Kook** (1891-1982).[1]

There are numerous stories about these two scholars, both of whom had a major impact on modern-day Israel. Why did I choose these particular stories? Each story displays a profound love for the Jewish people and the Land of Israel, a love which found natural expression in the actions and deeds of these saintly *tzaddikim*.

If there is an overriding trait to describe the multifaceted Rav Kook, it was his inner fountain of boundless, unquenchable love. A deep, profound love for his nation; a genuine love for all creatures; a mystical love for the Land of Israel; and an intense, blazing love for God. He saw no contradictions in these emotions. They poured out in his thoughts and speech, his essays and actions.

A scholarly biography might painstakingly research the dialectics of his philosophic approach, the ideological components of his Halakhic methodology, his public image, and his communal accomplishments – and yet fail to convey the core essence of his spirit and being, his authentic love of life, the universe, and its myriad beings. It is in the power of a story, however simple and unsophisticated, to communicate these qualities.

* * *

The incidents recorded in this book start from the year 1904, when Rav Kook left his native Latvia and accepted the position of Chief Rabbi of Jaffa and the surrounding *moshavot* (agricultural settlements).

---

[1] For an excellent account of Rav Kook's life, see: *An Angel Among Men* by Simcha Raz, translated by Rabbi Moshe Lichtman (Jerusalem: Kol Mevaser, 2003).

The stories are arranged in four sections. The first collection of stories took place during the decade that Rav Kook served as rabbi of Jaffa, from 1904 to 1914. This was a time of pioneering settlement and great hardship. *Eretz Yisrael* was under the rule of the Ottoman Empire, which was antagonistic to the growing Jewish community. These stories emphasize Rav Kook's ability to connect with the diverse Jewish communities in Palestine, especially the non-religious *halutzim* (pioneers) of the new settlements outside the major cities.

The stories of the second section are from the years 1914 to 1919. During those five years, Rav Kook was stranded in Europe when World War I broke out unexpectedly. He spent the first year and a half in Switzerland, where he met the young scholar who would become his most prominent disciple, Rabbi David Cohen, known as the "Rav HaNazir." The remaining years were spent in London, where he served as rabbi of the Mahzikei HaDath synagogue and had a hand in promoting the 1917 Balfour Declaration, which formally declared British support for a Jewish homeland in Palestine.

The third section starts in 1919 and ends with his death in 1935. The Great War was over, and Rav Kook was able to return to *Eretz Yisrael*. He accepted the position of Chief Rabbi of Jerusalem, and then established the Chief Rabbinate over all of pre-state Israel. The stories in this section reflect his approach to the complex issues of the time.

The final collection of stories in this book portrays Rav Kook's son, Rabbi Tzvi Yehudah HaKohen Kook. Shortly before his death, Rav Kook made two requests from his son: that he pay off all debts, and that he organize and publish his writings. Rav Tzvi Yehudah faithfully kept his promise. He dedicated his life to two major goals: publishing his father's extensive writings, and building up the Jerusalem yeshiva that his father had established in 1924, Mercaz HaRav.

Unlike the previous chapters, the incidents in this final section took place after the establishment of the State of Israel in 1948. Many of the stories shed light on Rav Tzvi Yehudah's role as a gifted educator, and the special rapport he enjoyed with the students in the yeshiva. They also reflect the historic upheaval that the Jewish people underwent, their transformation — after 2,000 years of dispersion and exile — into a sovereign nation, with the accompanying trials and challenges.

Rav Kook's writing desk in his modest study in Beit HaRav, the original location of the Mercaz HaRav yeshiva in Jerusalem.

Several years after his father's passing, Rav Tzvi Yehudah had a vision of his father in a dream, which he considered significant enough to relate to his students. After all, the Sages taught that dreams are a sixtieth part of prophecy. To some degree, this dream encapsulates the essence of Rav Kook's approach.

Rav Tzvi Yehudah dreamt he was in Jerusalem during a blackout in the 1948 War of Independence. It was a dangerous time; the Arab Legion was targeting the city with artillery and lethal sniper fire. Then he noticed that the lights were on in his father's study in the yeshiva.

Rav Tzvi Yehudah related:

I dreamt that it was wartime; artillery shells and blasts bombarded the city. And I saw my master and teacher, my father the Rav, of blessed memory. He was sitting and writing in his small workroom in the original building of the Mercaz HaRav yeshiva [on what is now HaRav Kook Street in downtown Jerusalem]. He was composing holy writings. The electric lights were lit, and they projected light outside the building.

But it was dangerous. The authorities gave strict orders for a blackout.

"Father," I said, "we must be careful. Perhaps we should cover the lamp? Or turn down the light?"

viii

"No," he replied. "There is no need to cover the lamps or reduce the light. The light will not cause any harm."

This reply, Rav Kook's response to the many dangers and upheavals of his generation, captures his essential message. Now is not the time to hide the light. On the contrary, we must add light! Our generation hungers for more light, for greater light. We must spread enlightenment and deepen our understanding of Torah and Judaism. *That* is our mission.[2]

* * *

Less than a year after Rav Kook's arrival in Jaffa, his beloved father-in-law passed away. Rabbi Eliyahu David Rabinowitz-Teomim (known as the "Aderet") was the Chief Rabbi of Jerusalem. Soon after, Rav Kook penned a spiritual biography of his father-in-law, entitled *Eider Hayakar.*[3] In the first chapter, parts of which are quoted in the following section, *The Value of a Story*, Rav Kook analyzed the positive impact of biographies of spiritual giants, particularly in a time when materialism and spiritual poverty are rampant.

Rabbi Eliyahu David Rabinowitz-Teomim, the Aderet (1843—1905) (Wikimedia Commons)

---

[2] As Rav Kook famously wrote in *Arpilei Tohar*, p. 39:
"The pure righteous do not complain about evil; rather they increase justice. They do not complain about godlessness, but increase faith.
They do not complain about ignorance, but increase wisdom."
[3] The book's name is based on Zechariah 11:13, which speaks of the redemption of Israel. The word *"eider"* ("magnificent") recalls the acronym of his father-in-law's name, the Aderet.

The first benefit is of a practical or educational nature. Such stories are a source of inspiration, encouraging the reader to imitate the character traits of *tzaddikim* and follow in their holy paths.

The second benefit, however, is even more remarkable. These stories have the ability to connect with the inner nobility of the reader's soul. Their poetry has the power to ignite the soul's inner spark and kindle its higher aspirations.

My hope is that these stories will succeed in inspiring you, the reader, and kindle the Divine spark within.

Chanan Morrison
Mitzpe Yericho, Israel
http://ravkooktorah.org

Acknowledgements

I would like to thank the following people for their contributions:

Tamar Rimon, for the reproduction of her beautiful oil on canvas painting of Rav Tzvi Yehudah Kook.

Rabbi Yikhat Rosen of the Or Eztion Institute, for his assistance in obtaining suitable photographs.

The copyright holder of the augmented edition of the biography *Harry Fischel, Pioneer of Jewish Philanthropy, Forty Years of Struggle for a Principle and the Years Beyond*, for permission to reproduce the photograph on page 79.

Rabbanit Dr. Naomi Cohen, for providing the photo of Haifa Chief Rabbi She'ar Yashuv Cohen in his study.

Rabbi Ze'ev Noyman, for use of photos of Rav Tzvi Yehudah from his collection (efforts were made to locate the copyright holders).

And of course, sincere thanks to my editor, **Sara Bonchek**, who greatly enhanced the work's quality with her insightful comments and painstaking corrections.

The Value of a Story

The following translation is from the first chapter of Eider Hayakar, *published by Rav Kook in Jaffa in 1906, following the passing of his father-in-law, the Aderet.*

When the goal of life, both material and spiritual, is reduced to the lowest level of base materialism, the nation is wracked with pain. Its breathing is arrested, its heartbeat becomes irregular, its organs are subject to seizures. *"Israel is compared to a bird"* (*Vayikra Rabbah* 11:18). The nation was destined to fly; and fly it must. *"Its heart and flesh will sing to the living God"* (based on Psalms 84:2).

But how can it take flight when its legs are mired in the mud? How can it fly when life is plagued by chaos and darkness, in contrast to a reign of spirit and nobility?

When desperation hits, Jacob[4] thinks to himself: perhaps this is now my fate – to slither on my belly and eat dirt? At this point, the people of Israel need to lift their eyes and look to the elders of the generation, the spiritual elite on whose knees they were raised. They should contemplate the majesty of their elders' lives and the grandeur of their aspirations.

In these elders, they will recognize their own inner spirit, for the nation's spirit is revealed in its greatest citizens. Then they will realize the inner content of their own lives.

* * *

---

[4] i.e. the Jewish people.

The value of telling the stories of *tzaddikim* of Israel is profound. Its value is in measure with the impact of the amazing sight – that of the life of a man of spirit, who transcended life's petty aspects, who lives exclusively in an atmosphere of holiness and purity, justice and integrity....

Knowing the history of a remarkable individual provides both practical and theoretical benefits. The practical benefit is similar to the principle that *"The envy of scholars increases wisdom"* (*Baba Batra* 21a). When one perceives the splendor of holiness and inner beauty that a great individual attained, he is inspired to try his hand at following that individual's path. Even if one is unable to fully emulate him, it is impossible not to be moved to some extent to ascend from one's lowly state to a loftier level. One is inspired to adopt some examples of his ethical conduct and precious accomplishments, especially when one realizes the tremendous efforts the protagonist made to attain them.

And the theoretical benefit: the soul's innate nobility blossoms like a flower when exposed to a lofty and glorious spectacle. The very sight of spiritual greatness uplifts the spirit and refines the heart, even if it is inconceivable to actually imitate that which is so much higher and loftier.... Even when merely contemplating such an image, we bask in its precious light.

Completing the task [of writing a spiritual biography] is difficult. It is especially difficult when dealing with our remarkable genius, of blessed memory....

Jaffa

1904-1914

Timeline	for Rabbi Abraham Isaac HaKohen Kook
1865	Born in Grieve, Latvia.
1884-1885	Studied at the famed Volozhin yeshiva under Rabbi Naftali Tzvi Berlin, the "Netziv" (age 18-19).
1888	Appointed rabbi of Zeimel in Lithuania (age 22-31).
1896	Appointed rabbi of Boisk, Latvia (age 31-38).
1904-1914	Arrived in *Eretz Yisrael*, serving as rabbi of Jaffa and surrounding settlements for the next decade (age 38-49).
1913	Led a mission of rabbis to settlements in the north (age 48).
1914-1915	Stranded in Switzerland for over a year during WWI; met Rabbi David Cohen, the "Rav HaNazir" (age 49-50).
1916-1919	Served for three years as rabbi of the Mahzikei HaDath congregation in London (age 51-54).
1919	Returned to *Eretz Yisrael*, elected Chief Rabbi of Jerusalem (age 54).
1921	Elected Chief Rabbi of *Eretz Yisrael* (age 56).
1924	Established the Mercaz HaRav yeshiva in Jerusalem (age 59).
1935	Passed away in Jerusalem on the third of Elul, two weeks before his 70th birthday.

RAV KOOK ARRIVES IN JAFFA

As the steamship from Odessa entered the Jaffa harbor, brightly lit by the morning sun of early summer, Rav Kook peered out over the dark blue Mediterranean waters and studied the picturesque port town and its stone buildings.

For the past sixteen years, Rav Kook had served as the local rabbi in small Jewish communities in Latvia and Lithuania. Recently he had been offered a lucrative post as *mashgiah ruhani*, the spiritual dean, of a highly respected yeshiva in Lithuania – an opportunity to have a major impact on the lives of the next generation's leaders.

Yet he had turned down the offer, accepting instead a much more problematic position: Chief Rabbi of the rough and gritty town of Jaffa, with its deeply divided Jewish community, where religious and secular, Ashkenazim and Sephardim, Hasidim and Mitnagdim, struggled and fought one another under the adverse rule of the Ottoman Empire.

The previous rabbi of Jaffa had passed away two years earlier. Rabbi Yoel Moshe Solomon, a pioneering figure in Jerusalem and one of the founders of Petah Tikva, was among the first to suggest offering the Jaffa position to Rav Kook. Rabbi Solomon brought the proposal to the Chief Rabbi of Jerusalem – Rav Kook's father-in-law – Rabbi Eliyahu David Rabinowitz-Teomim, the "Aderet."

That same day, the Aderet sent an urgent message to his son-in-law, advising him to accept the position of rabbi of Jaffa and its surrounding communities. Rav Kook was excited by the proposal, but wanted to know what Rabbi Shmuel Salant, the previous Chief Rabbi of Jerusalem and its elder statesman, thought about the proposal. The Aderet reported that when he queried Rabbi Salant, the elderly scholar happily responded, "If only!"

The Aderet noted with irony: "In truth, my son-in-law should have been appointed the rabbi of the holy city of Jerusalem, and I should have been the rabbi of the small town of Jaffa." In fact, fifteen years later Rav Kook *did* become the Chief Rabbi of Jerusalem.

Despite the entreaties of the townspeople of Boisk that their beloved rabbi not leave, and despite the tempting offer to serve as a yeshiva dean, Rav Kook saw in the Jaffa position a fulfillment of his long-cherished dream to live in *Eretz Yisrael.*

His parents recalled that, even as a small child, their son had exhibited exuberant passion for the Land of Israel. In the local *heider*, he invented a new game for his classmates. During recess, the children would line up with their satchels on their shoulders, and young Abraham Isaac would bark, "Where are we going?"

"To the Land of Israel!" his friends would roar in reply.

And so, in the early summer of 1904, the Kook family left their home in Boisk, traveling to Riga, and from there to Dvinsk and then Odessa. In Odessa, they boarded a steamship which carried them, after an arduous twelve-day voyage, to Jaffa. Rav Kook had at last fulfilled his childhood dream – *"to the Land of Israel!"*

On the Jaffa beach, the local community waited to greet their new rabbi. Rabbi Yoel Moshe Solomon, together with other public figures who had worked to bring Rav Kook to Jaffa, set out in a small rowboat to meet the steamship.

The weekly newspaper *HaHashkafah* described the occasion:

> On Friday, the 28th of Iyyar, our new rabbi made his appearance in our town.... He was received with great honor by residents of the community from all sections of the population. Messengers came from Jerusalem to welcome him in the name of Rabbi Shmuel Salant and the Aderet. Delegates also came from the agricultural settlements of Rishon Letzion, Petah Tikvah, and so on, to receive their new rabbi.

Important representatives from the Sephardic community also arrived, and he spoke with them in pure Hebrew. It is rare to find an [Ashkenazi] rabbi who can speak such a pure, flowing Hebrew. On the Sabbath morning, the rabbi spoke well with a clear, unadulterated Hebrew; and the Sephardic Jews were also able to understand his words and enjoy the sermon.

Even the Chabad Hasidim expressed their opinion that they consider the new rabbi to be the best possible choice. They concluded that such a rabbi was on par with the rabbis of the greatest cities of the world, due to his great wisdom and erudition.... They also consoled themselves that even though the new rabbi was educated in non-Hasidic yeshivot, on his mother's side he is descended from Chabad Hasidim, and is endowed with several Hasidic qualities.

Rav Kook's exceptional appeal to all sectors of the city is reflected in the picturesque testimony of "the artist of early Tel Aviv," Nahum Gutman. Gutman's family arrived in Jaffa in 1905, and he spent his childhood living close to Rav Kook's home in Jaffa's Neve Tzedek neighborhood. He wrote:

Rav Kook's house was a few hundred steps from our home. His house was enclosed with a whitewashed fence. The courtyard had a gate and contained a small garden and a well of water.

Just the sight of the house conveyed an atmosphere of serenity and joy. Through the open windows of the house, we could hear the sounds of Jews studying Torah.

And when the figure of Rav Kook would appear at the gate, as he readied himself to walk to synagogue – this image would always take my breath away.

As a child I adored him, with his graceful beauty, his noble serenity, and his unwavering poise. His persona fascinated me so much that I would literally follow after him, placing my feet in the footprints that he left in the sand....

I never met another man like that, a rabbi who knew how to attract people from all sectors and factions. What a personality he was!

Neve Tzedek wall painting of Jaffa intellectuals in the early 1900s.
From right: Rav Kook, Shmuel Yosef Agnon, David Shimoni, Alexander Ziskind Rabinowitz (Azar), Yosef Haim Brenner. (Photo credit: Dr. Avishai Teicher/PikiWiki)

THE BLESSING OF A KOHEN

Rav Kook's duties as Chief Rabbi of Jaffa and the surrounding settlements were demanding and complex. In order to rest from the long hours and the pressures of the position, Rav Kook would go on vacation in the late summer, staying in the agricultural settlement of Rehovot during the peak of the grape harvest season.[5]

In a letter written in 1910, Rav Kook expressed his joy at seeing the *moshavah* grow and flourish:

> I am currently residing in Rehovot (may it be built up and established). I am completely enthralled by Godly hopes and consolations, as I see with my own eyes the development of our precious land which was desolate, and is now cultivated by the hands of our brethren once scattered throughout the Exile, who are slowly returning. My heart rejoices at the sight of peaceful dwellings, delightful vineyards, the beauty of the grape and the fig and the pomegranate, in the fields of our people, in the place of [Zion], the very source of our lives. (*Letters* vol. I, p. 359)

---

[5] During his stay in England during World War I, Rav Kook traveled to the spa town of Harrogate, where his doctor insisted he spend time each day touring its famous parks and gardens. In an attempt to raise the rabbi's spirits, his assistant, Rabbi Glitzenstein, noted the park's beautiful views and landscapes.

"But it is not Rehovot," Rav Kook responded sadly. "In Rehovot's holy and beloved vistas, I could take pleasure. But what connection do I have to these foreign lands, over which a foreign spirit hovers?"

But even in Rehovot, it was not a simple matter for Rav Kook to rest. The local residents were thrilled to host the revered scholar. They sought out his advice, not only in Halakhic matters, but also in local administrative issues – municipal tax collection, paving local roads, and so forth. And if a Torah subject was broached, Rav Kook became an overflowing wellspring of knowledge and creativity; he would often expound on a topic for hours.

In Rehovot, Rav Kook would stay in the modest home of the Lipkovitz family. Abraham Isaac Lipkovitz, who worked in construction and agriculture, had studied Torah in European yeshivot before making *aliyah* with his family at age 18. He took upon himself to facilitate his esteemed guest's rest and recuperation.

Lipkovitz took this duty most seriously and formulated an appropriate plan. He zealously watched over the Rav's meals and sleep, adamantly preventing anyone from disturbing him while he slept, no matter what the occasion.

But it quickly became apparent that in the Lipkovitz home and in the synagogue, where Rav Kook was constantly badgered with queries and solicitations, the rabbi could not properly rest.

The Lipkovitz's owned a vineyard, one that produced some of the choicest grapes in the country. Lipkovitz built a simple hut inside the vineyard for Rav Kook's personal use. Each day, he would lead Rav Kook to the vineyard on a donkey. And for two hours, Rav Kook would rest in the hut.

Lipkovitz probably assumed that the rabbi spent this quiet time resting, eating grapes, and reading light material. In fact, Rav Kook's mind was far away from Rehovot and its bountiful vineyards. His thoughts soared to the rarified heights of Lithuanian Torah scholarship. He utilized those precious hours of peace and quiet to engage in serious research, producing an erudite commentary to the glosses of the famed Rabbi Elijah, the Gaon of Vilna, on the *Shulchan Aruch*. This scholarly work, *Be'er Eliyahu (Elijah's Well)*, elucidates the Gaon's terse hints and novel ideas on Halakhah and Talmud.

Many years later, during his final illness, Rav Kook described his feeling of profound privilege when working on this project. "When I was writing *Be'er Eliyahu*, I felt as if I was standing in the very presence of the Gaon of Vilna. It was as if I was presenting to him the books — the Babylonian and Jerusalem Talmuds, the works of Maimonides and the other *Rishonim* [rabbinic authorities from the 11th to 15th centuries]." Rav Kook's eyes flowed with tears. "I thank God for the great honor of serving our master, the Gaon, to a small degree."

Visitors would frequently arrive from Jaffa or Jerusalem in order to consult with Rav Kook. They were allowed to accompany him on the trip to the vineyard. But once they reached the vineyard, they were barred from entering. Lipkovitz gave strict orders to his Arab watchman not to allow any visitors to disturb the rabbi.

Lipkovitz was overjoyed with the privilege of serving Rav Kook. He also had a modest request of the rabbi, a request which took him time until he succeeded in bringing it up with his esteemed guest. Lipkovitz related:

> Rav Kook stayed at my house, and I very much wanted to receive a blessing from him. But the Rav was always absorbed in his Torah studies, or he had visitors, and I dared not interrupt.
>
> One day I noticed that the Rav had raised his eyes from the Torah text he was studying. At the time I was holding some chickens in my hands. I immediately released the chickens and dashed to the Rav in order to present my request.
>
> "*You* need a blessing?" the Rav replied in surprise. "After all, you merited to ascend to the Land of Israel and live in the Holy Land with financial security."
>
> The Rav paused for a moment. "Nonetheless, I am a *kohen*; and it is a mitzvah for me to bless the Jewish people at all times."

> Rav Kook then blessed me that I would merit a long
> life – *arichut yamim* – until the time of the Redemption.

"From that time on," Lipkovitz remarked, "I lived in tranquility, placing my faith in the scholar's blessing."

After the Six-Day War in 1967, when the Old City of Jerusalem was liberated and the borders of Israel were expanded, Lipkovitz began to worry. Perhaps the Rav's blessing has already been fulfilled? Perhaps his hour had arrived?

In fact, Abraham Isaac Lipkovitz lived many more years. He finally passed away at the ripe old age of 108. Until his death, he was known as *zekan hayishuv*, "the community elder." Over the years, when people asked him how he had merited such a long life, he would reply with simplicity, "Why, I have a blessing from Rav Kook!"

The main road in Rehovot, 1912

THE HETTER MEKHIRAH FOR THE SABBATICAL YEAR

As Jews began returning to *Eretz Yisrael* and settling the land in the late 1800s, establishing farms and *moshavot*, the question of letting fields lie fallow during the Sabbatical year became – for the first time in many centuries – a burning issue. How could the newly established farming communities survive an entire year without cultivating their fields? How could the farmers survive an entire year without any income from their crops and orchards?

With the approach of the Sabbatical year in 1889, the Jewish farmers turned to the rabbis to issue a *hetter*, a permit, that would allow them to continue working their lands during the seventh year and prevent the collapse of their fragile agricultural enterprises.

In response, three respected scholars met in Vilna and designed a *hetter mekhirah*, which temporarily sold the land to a non-Jew over the Sabbatical year. The *hetter* was approved by Rabbi Yitzchak Elchanan Spector, Chief Rabbi of Kovno and the pre-eminent Halakhic authority of the time.

During the following Sabbatical years of 1896 and 1903, many of the new agricultural settlements utilized the *hetter*. However, a number of highly respected scholars vociferously opposed the leniency. Among the opponents were the Beit HaLevy (Rabbi Yosef Dov Soloveitchik), the Netziv (Rabbi Naftali Zvi Yehudah Berlin, head of the Volozhin yeshiva), and Rabbi Samson Raphael Hirsch.

Leading up to the Sabbatical year of 1910, Rav Kook, as Chief Rabbi of Jaffa and the surrounding *moshavot*, took a forceful position defending the *hetter mekhirah*. He penned a treatise entitled *Shabbat Ha'Aretz*, which explained the legal reasoning behind the permit, along with a discussion of the laws of the Sabbatical year.

25

While Rav Kook was an original and creative thinker, he usually took a conservative position on issues of Jewish law. What lead him to support the lenient position in the *hetter mekhirah* controversy?

Much about his motives and underlying concerns can be gleaned from letters that he wrote during this time period, letters later published in the first volume of *Igrot HaRe'iyah*.

Supporting the *Hetter*

While still in Russia, Rav Kook and his father-in-law, the Aderet (then rabbi of Ponevezh), analyzed the issue at length. In his letters, Rav Kook revealed that at that time they both opposed the *hetter*.

> From afar, when we heard the arguments of those who permit and of those who forbid, we both leaned toward the stricter opinion. But when the Aderet arrived in the Land of Israel, he saw with his own eyes that it is impossible to even consider not providing some sort of arrangement for the Sabbatical year. (p. 258)

Seeing the precarious state of the agricultural settlements first-hand was a critical factor in changing Rav Kook's mind. He understood that full observance of the Sabbatical year could endanger lives and would likely bring about the economic collapse of the new settlements.

An even greater worry was that the entire enterprise of the Jewish people's return to the Land of Israel could founder over this issue. At that time, the nascent economy of the Yishuv in *Eretz Yisrael* was based on the commercial sale and export of agricultural produce:

> The JCA [Jewish Colonial Association] representative informed me that the JCA is preparing plans to buy much more property in the Holy Land. But if we decide that there is no permit to allow work during the seventh year via some legal sale, then the representative

will be forced to advise the JCA to invest their money in Canada, and cease supporting [projects in] the Land of Israel. He also said that [if the land lays fallow during the Sabbatical year], the Arabs will take control of Jewish land during the Sabbatical year by grazing their herds on them, and it will be necessary to take them to court. (p. 285)

A third concern – one that was obviously deeply disturbing for Rav Kook – was his fear that a strict ruling would demonstrate to all that Judaism is incompatible with the modern world and the building of a Jewish state. He wrote:

Even worse is the potential condemnation of Judaism and widespread rejection of Torah observance that could result from a strict ruling, Heaven forbid. For the anti-religious elements actually hope that the rabbis will forbid [all agricultural activity during the Sabbatical year]. Then they will have gained a great victory. They will have demonstrated that by following the rabbis, the land will be laid waste, the fields and vineyards will become desolate, and all commercial ties for the export of wine, oranges, and other produce will be broken – ties upon which the survival of the Jewish settlement truly depends. (p. 258)

Legal Underpinnings

In his letters, Rav Kook also discussed the legal reasoning behind the *hetter mekhirah*. The sale is actually based on a number of independent, mitigating factors, each one lessening the severity of working the land during the Sabbatical year.

The most important factor in taking a lenient stance is the ruling of the majority of Halakhic authorities that nowadays, since most Jews do the Land of Israel, the Sabbatical year no longer retains the iblical law. Because it is rabbinically ordained, we may apply various leniencies, according to the well-known principle of *sfeika d'rabbanan lekula*.

Furthermore, the *hetter* only permits those categories of agricultural labor which are not Biblically prohibited, even when the Sabbatical year itself is Biblically ordained. Thus, planting, pruning, harvesting, fruit-picking, and perhaps plowing must still be performed by non-Jews hired to work the field, and not by the Jewish farmers themselves. This clause ensures that no Torah prohibitions are violated, even according to the minority opinion that nowadays the Sabbatical year is Biblically ordained.

An additional reason to be lenient is that the situation was one of "undue hardship" (*sha'at hadechak*). Given the precarious state of the agricultural settlements, not working the land would be truly life-threatening. In such cases, one may rely on a single opinion – that of Rabbi Zerahiah HaLevi Gerondi – who held that nowadays, without the Jubilee year, the Sabbatical year is not even rabbinically ordained, but is only a pious custom.[6]

Rav Kook intimated that he had additional reasons to be lenient, but intentionally did not publicize them. He feared that, once institutionalized, the *hetter* would become *too* entrenched. The ultimate goal was not to circumvent the laws of the Sabbatical year, but to allow the settlements to grow and prosper until they would be able to completely observe the Sabbatical year in all of its details.

---

[6] Rav Kook also took into account the doubt regarding the correct count of the years. The *Kaftor Vaferach* (Rabbi Eshtori HaParchi, 1282-1357) testified that some farmers would observe the seventh year during one year, while others observed it during another. Even though the rabbis agreed to observe just one Sabbatical year (and Maimonides' count was chosen), this is only a convention; the doubt still remains as to which year is truly the Sabbatical year.

On purpose, I did not organize everything in this matter to be fully explained, organized, and analyzed as it should be. Some justifications and cogent arguments I have omitted completely. All this was in order that the *hetter* should not become too accepted, but will always be considered a temporary measure (*hora'at sha'ah*), something that was permitted grudgingly due to the needs of the time. But when these issues are analyzed in the way of true Torah scholarship... the prohibition would become too weakened – and I certainly did not seek that outcome.... (pp. 348-349)

Many of the rabbis who opposed the *hetter mekhirah* wrote that not observing the Sabbatical year would in fact jeopardize the future of Jewish settlement in the Land of Israel, for the Sages taught that the punishment for violating its laws is exile (*Avot* 5:9). While Rav Kook looked forward to the day when the Sabbatical year would be fully observed, he viewed the *hetter* as a stepping-stone that would allow the nation to achieve that goal:

We are obligated to strive with all of our strength to bring matters so that, in the end, the Sabbatical year will be increasingly observed in all of its holiness in the Holy Land.... But how to arrive at this sacred goal? Which means should we use to attain it? This matter must be considered carefully.

In my opinion, we need to arrive at our desired goal precisely by graduated efforts. Rabbi Hiyya Rabbah described the overall redemption of Israel as beginning slowly, little by little [Jerusalem Talmud, *Berachot* 1:2]. So, too, the spiritual redemption of establishing the Land's holiness will advance in stages, step by step. (p. 330)

One expression of this graduated approach is the distinction the *hetter* made between those agricultural activities that are prohibited Biblically and those prohibited rabbinically. "We should be like one who rescues his possessions from the fire," Rav Kook explained. "Whatever is more precious and holier [i.e., Biblically prohibited actions] must be rescued first."

What about those who did not wish to rely on the *hetter mekhirah*? Here, Rav Kook distinguished between farmers and consumers. He was very supportive of farmers who did not wish to rely on the *hetter*. When he heard that the JCA was using the *hetter* to force farmers to work during the Sabbatical year, he became acutely distressed, and threatened the JCA that the *hetter* would become invalid under such circumstances. Rav Kook also promoted the establishment of a special fund to support these farmers.

On the other hand, Rav Kook deplored the phenomenon of consumers who chose to be stringent in the Sabbatical year by buying produce only from non-Jewish farmers. One cannot adopt stringencies (*humrot*), he warned, at the expense of others.

> It is certainly improper to look for leniencies and loopholes by purchasing produce from non-Jews, in a situation when this will cause loss of income to Jewish farmers and undermine their livelihood. In general, whenever one desires to be strict for himself, it is proper to make certain that this stringency does not bring about any negative repercussions of financial loss or disrepute for others. (p. 258)

Despite Rav Kook's best efforts, there was significant rabbinical opposition to the *hetter mekhirah*. In particular, the elderly rabbi of Safed, Rabbi Yaakov David Willowsky, fought tooth and nail against any form of permit allowing agricultural labor during the Sabbatical year. Convinced that Rav Kook's support of the *hetter* was due to heavy pressure from the JCA and anti-religious Zionists, he

30

offered to help Rav Kook find an appropriate rabbinical post outside the country. Then, he reasoned, Rav Kook would be free to backtrack on his support for the *hetter*.

In his response, Rav Kook expressed shock and dismay at the very thought of leaving the Land of Israel. Expressing his profound love for the Land, he replied:

> I was particularly astounded by your suggestion to leave the Land of Israel for a rabbinical position outside the country. In truth, if I were presented with all the treasures of the world, at the price of one moment of breathing the holy air of *Eretz Yisrael* – I would not accept. And conversely, if I were offered all the gold and silver in the world for a single breath of the impure air of foreign lands, I would scorn and reject the offer. (*Letters*, vol. II, p. 154)

Ploughing a field in the Galilee, 1913

THE VISIT TO MERHAVYA

"You speak of desecration of Torah and mitzvot?" Abraham Isaac Lipkovitz exploded. "Rabbis. are firefighters! Go put out the fires! What are you doing sitting around here?"

A group of rabbis, including Rav Kook, had gathered in Lipkovitz's home in Rehovot to discuss the state of religious life in the Land of Israel. They were particularly disturbed by blatant violations of the Sabbath in the new settlements.

But Lipkovitz, who worked in construction and agriculture, was a doer. He had little patience for the rabbis' endless discussions. He cited the example of the prophet Samuel, who would travel around the country to fortify religious observance.

"You rabbis are sitting here, while over there – there are fires burning! Every day, the fires destroy more and more. And you are responsible! You are at fault!" Lipkovitz took a breath. "You need to go to all these places and demand that the Sabbath be observed."

For several years, Rav Kook had toyed with the idea of a rabbinical tour of the northern communities. Perhaps it was Lipkovitz's outburst which spurred the rabbi to put his plan into action.

In mid-November of 1913, a small delegation of rabbis, led by Rav Kook, set out to visit the new communities of the Galilee and the north. The rabbinical tour was meant to strengthen ties with the isolated *moshavot* and bolster religious observance. Rav Kook delineated the tour's objectives in his introduction to *Eileh Massei*, a pamphlet which documented the rabbis' month-long tour:

> We are called upon to assist as best we can, *"to come to God's aid for the heroes"* (Judges 5:23) – to visit the *moshavot*, to raise their spirits, to inject the dew of holy

life into the bones of the settlements… [We must] elevate the life of faithful Judaism, and publicly announce the call for harmony and unity between the Old Yishuv [the established religious communities in the cities] and the New Yishuv [the new Zionist settlements].

The journey enabled the rabbis to meet the pioneers of the First and Second Aliyah, and learn of the difficulties of life on the *moshavot* first-hand. In fact, meeting and interacting with Rav Kook, the elderly Rabbi Yosef Chaim Zonnenfeld of Jerusalem, and the other rabbis in the delegation had a powerful impact on many of the pioneers. In many cases it succeeded in awakening a desire for greater observance of the Sabbath and kashruth. Practical arrangements for separating agricultural tithes were instituted, and other religious matters were worked out.

Rabbi Yosef Chaim Zonnenfeld (1849-1932) (Zionist Archives, Wikimedia Commons)

But the most crucial issue – the lack of traditional Jewish education for the children – could not be properly addressed during such a short visit.

* * *

The cooperative settlement Merhavya had been established two years earlier, in 1911. It was the first Jewish settlement in the desolate Jezreel valley, near Afula. Members of *HaShomer,* an early Jewish defense organization, protected the settlement from attacks by Bedouin and neighboring Arabs.

Gershon Gafner, a prominent member of the cooperative, recorded his memories of the rabbis' visit in his memoir, *My Path to Merhavya*:

We were informed of the arrival date for the visit of Rabbis Kook and Zonnenfeld, of blessed memory, and Rabbi Yadler. In honor of these esteemed guests, we hired a "diligence" [a French stagecoach] from Nazareth to bring them from the Afula station to Merhavya. The visit, however, was postponed repeatedly. Since it was expensive to retain the diligence coach, we had to return this elegant and modern (for those days) form of transportation.

One day we were surprised to receive an urgent message from Afula. The rabbis had arrived and were waiting for us at the station! We were to come at once and bring them to Merhavya.

Lacking a better option, we quickly "renovated" one of the carts which we used to transport manure. We cleaned it up, "upholstered" it with straw and sacks, and made our way to Afula. In this fashion, we brought our honored guests to Merhavya....

We expressed our regret that we did not have the opportunity on such short notice – from when we learned of their arrival – to prepare a more suitable form of transportation for them. In response to this apology, Rav Kook delivered an impassioned speech. His fiery address lasted nearly an hour.

Rav Kook expressed his great joy that, for the first time in his life, he was privileged to travel in a wagon of Jewish laborers in the Land of the Patriarchs. His speech probed the depths of Jewish history. He praised the importance of working the land and recalled the sacred history of the Jezreel valley, which we pioneers were the first to redeem after centuries of desolation. With tremendous excitement, he noted that our fathers' fathers had lived in this place, creating Jewish life with dedication and self-sacrifice. And now, he noted, the descendants of those ancient Hebrews have arisen and continued their Jewish tradition.

He concluded his words with a heartfelt blessing that we should merit to see, with our own eyes, the entire Land of Israel redeemed and flourishing through the labor of the children of the Eternal Nation.

Rav Kook's words made a deep impression on us. We felt, with great admiration, that he was truly worthy of the crown of Torah that he wore.

The rabbinical delegation stayed with us several days. During one of the nights, the rabbis were witness to an attack on Merhavya. We explained to them that the Arabs primarily chose to attack us on Friday nights [on the assumption that few or no Jewish guards would be on duty]. Therefore we are forced to go out on the Sabbath to protect our property and our lives. We asked the rabbis to provide a clear answer if we are acting properly according to Jewish law.

Rav Kook responded calmly and with full understanding of the situation. If, he explained, we are certain that it is a life-threatening situation, then it is our *obligation* to defend the place, even if this will lead to violation of the Sabbath laws. This is in accordance with the well-known Halakhic principle, "Danger to human life overrides the laws of the Sabbath."

Rabbi Zonnenfeld, Rabbi Yadler, and the other rabbis, however, did not express an opinion one way or the other.

After his visit to Merhavya, Rav Kook closely followed after the development of the settlement. And the people of Merhavya – most of whom were far removed from traditional Judaism – felt a profound admiration for him. They saw in Rav Kook a Torah scholar blessed with a sensitive soul, as well as a broad and humane outlook.

DANCES OF TESHUVAH IN PORIAH

Avraham Rosenblatt was eighteen years old when he ran away from his parent's home in Kishinev. His parents objected to Avraham's dream to leave Russia for Palestine, as life under the oppressive rule of the Ottoman Empire was difficult and dangerous. So the young man, active for many years in a local Zionist youth group, quietly stole away from home and made his way to *Eretz Yisrael*.

Some decades later, Rosenblatt was a highly respected accountant and comptroller in Tel Aviv. But when he first came to the country, he was employed in the *moshavot* of the Galilee area as a farm hand and security guard for the *Hashomer* organization.

In the winter of 1913, Rosenblatt was working in Poriah, a small community near the Sea of Galilee, just south of Tiberius. Poriah was a fledgling agricultural community recently established by a group of forty young pioneers from St. Louis, Missouri. The *moshavah* was eventually abandoned several years later, after relentless confiscations and harassment by the Turks during World War I. Forty years would pass before the village of Poriah was re-established.

A high point in the short history of Poriah took place one November evening in 1913. Many of the pioneers present, including Rosenblatt, cherished the memory of that wonderful winter night, when the young secular pioneers sang and danced with the Chief Rabbi of Jaffa.

The pioneers of Poriah heard that Rav Kook was leading a rabbinical delegation to visit the remote Jewish settlements in the northern part of the country. When they learned that the delegation was close by, they sent two representatives – on the Sabbath! – to invite the rabbis to visit their community. Since Poriah was beyond the Sabbath limits, and thus it would have been forbidden for them to

36

return to Poriah, even on foot, Rav Kook did not provide an immediate answer. He wanted to prevent any further Sabbath desecration. Instead, he told the Poriah pioneers that if they waited until the Sabbath was over, he would give them his response. After reciting the *Havdalah* prayer at the end of the Sabbath, Rav Kook agreed to visit the following evening.

The visit to Poriah made a powerful impression on the young pioneers, who felt distant from rabbis and were estranged from religion in general. Rav Kook spoke to them about Jewish values and the mitzvah of settling the Land. He spoke of the need to unite the entire nation with a connection of souls and spirits.

"We need," the rabbi proclaimed, "to bind together all Jews, from the elderly rabbi of Jerusalem, Rabbi Zonnenfeld, to the youngest laborer of Poriah."

The pioneers responded with cheers and applause. Full of youthful enthusiasm, the young men jumped up and danced with Rav Kook.

* * *

We are fortunate to possess Avraham Rosenblatt's testimony of that evening. In a letter written nearly sixty years after the event, he described in detail the stirring encounter, vividly etched in his memory:

> I recall a beautiful episode that took place 57 years ago, when Rav Kook toured the *moshavot* in the Galilee. I was working in the Poriah farm near the town of Tiberius. At the time we were just a handful of sixty workers. In the end of Tishrei, 5674, we heard that Rav Kook, together with three other rabbis – Rabbis Zonnenfeld, Yadler, and Horowitz – were touring the isolated *moshavot* in the Galilee in order to influence them to greater religious observance and purity.
>
> I remember that we were told that the delegation was staying nearby, and that the rabbis would also visit

Poriah. We sat in the dining hall, singing and dancing, as was our custom back then. Then we heard that the delegation had arrived in Poriah and was in the office of the manager, Eliyahu Israelite, and that the rabbis wished to meet with us.

We had already finished eating. We were dancing and singing, *"God will rebuild the Galilee,"* when Rav Kook joined in and danced with the men.

Suddenly Rav Kook turned to me and my friend, Pinhas Schneerson. We were both on guard duty that night; we were wearing Arab cloaks and kefiyyeh headdresses, with rifles slung on our shoulders. Rav Kook asked us to accompany him to the manager's office. I was shorter than the rabbi, but Schneerson was tall, so Rav Kook asked Schneerson if he could borrow his "uniform."

The three of us returned to the dancing, with the Rav wearing a kefiyyeh on his head and a rifle over his shoulder. Everyone stared at Rav Kook's change of dress. The truth is, the clothes suited him. The Rav began to sing a song from the liturgy, *"Vetaheir Libeinu"* – "Purify our hearts, so that we may truly serve You."

Then the rabbi stopped and spoke to us. "Dear brothers! Holy brothers! Builders of the Land! Just as I am not embarrassed to wear your garments, so too, I request – do not be embarrassed by the Torah of Israel! In the merit of observing the Torah's mitzvot, you will live many years in the Land of Israel, in sanctity and purity, in the study of the holy Torah. Is it so hard to be a Jew? In your homes in the Diaspora, you were certainly educated in the spirit of Judaism. Your homes were conducted in purity and religious observance. Please, please...."

Rav Kook concluded his address with the following request: "I will not remove the uniform of your guard unless you promise me – all of you, with one heart and a willing soul – that you will fulfill my request. I ask that *you* should be guards: that you guard over your *pintele yid*, your inner Jewish spark."

We all cried out, "We promise!"

And the Rav responded, "Happy is the eye that witnessed such dances of *teshuvah* [repentance] and holiness. Praised be God's name!"

Rav Kook then went to the manager's office and quickly returned to join in our dancing. He sang "*Vekariev pizureinu*" – "Bring home our dispersed from among the nations" – and other such songs. The Rav continued to dance and sing with us for over an hour.

The delegation remained the following day to oversee the kashering of all the kitchen utensils. They instructed the young women working in the kitchen in the laws of kosher food; and the rabbis departed in joy and happiness.

Another worker who was present that evening, Ze'ev Horowitz of Kibbutz Geva, recalled the happy exuberance and high spirits:

I will never forget that image: Rav Kook, a tall, handsome man with a high hat, spied a security guard wearing a Bedouin cloak. He said, "Let's exchange – I'll take your 'rabbinical cloak,' and you'll take mine."

Oh, how our spirits soared!

At the end, the Rav announced, "I wore your clothes, and you wore mine. So it should also be on the *inside* – together in our hearts!"

39

Jewish guards wearing Arab cloaks and headdresses, 1915

Europe

1914-1919

Rav Kook in London, 1917 (Beit HaRav Archives, Jerusalem)

Rabbi David Cohen, the Rav HaNazir (1887-1972)

THE NAZIR OF JERUSALEM

Rav Kook's most prominent disciple was the scholar and mystic Rabbi David Cohen. He was known as the "Rav HaNazir" (or "the Nazir of Jerusalem"), since he conducted himself as a Nazarite, never drinking wine, eating grapes, or cutting his hair. The Rav HaNazir edited and organized many of Rav Kook's writings into the four-volume magnum opus, *Orot HaKodesh*.

Who was this scholar? How did he meet Rav Kook?

David Cohen was a yeshiva student from the Vilna area blessed with exceptional intellectual talents. He studied in Raduń under the famed scholar Rabbi Israel Meir Kagan, known as the Chafetz Chaim. Cohen attended the leading yeshivot of the day, including Volozhin and Slabodka. After preparing himself for matriculation exams, he was accepted to the University of Basel in Switzerland, where he studied philosophy and classical literature for seven years.

However, the 26-year-old student was not at peace with himself. While he rose early every morning for prayers and carefully observed mitzvoth, he felt something was missing and suffered from an inner discontent.

When Cohen heard that Rav Kook was staying in St. Gallen, Switzerland, after becoming stranded in Europe due to the unexpected outbreak of the First World War – the rabbi had left *Eretz Yisrael* to attend a major rabbinical conference in Frankfurt – the hopeful young scholar sent off a letter to Rav Kook: Would it be possible to discuss various matters of faith?

Cohen was overjoyed when he received a positive reply. Lacking the means to pay for the trip, he handed over his gold watch to a local pawnshop to raise the necessary funds.

Cohen prepared himself by performing a ritual immersion in the Rhine River; then he set off for St. Gallen. It was the start of the autumn month of Elul, a time of introspection and repentance preceding the High Holidays.

Rav Kook received the young scholar warmly. They spoke, mainly about Greek philosophy and literature, the entire day. Rav Kook was struck by the expertise his visitor demonstrated on these topics in their original sources. Cohen, on the other hand, felt disappointed. Had he come all this way, even pawning his watch, just to discuss Greek philosophy?

Rav Kook suggested that the young man stay overnight. Reluctantly, Cohen agreed. The entire night, he tossed and turned, unable to sleep. What would be tomorrow? Would Rav Kook resolve his questions? Would he succeed in dispelling his doubts? He felt his life's destiny was hanging in the balance. Which way would it go?

As the first rays of morning light broke through the window, the young man heard footsteps from the adjoining room. That must be the Rav, he thought. He must be praying. What is he saying?

He heard Rav Kook chant the *Akeidah*, the Biblical account of Isaac's binding, a story of ultimate love and self-sacrifice. The melody captivated his heart. Then the rabbi recited the concluding supplication, *"Ribono shel olam! Master of the World, may it be Your will... that You recall for our sake the covenant of our fathers...."* The sweetness and exhilarating fervor in Rav Kook's prayer shook the very foundations of the young man's soul.

This inspiring *tefilah*, recited in holiness and purity, changed him. Many years later, he tersely described this transformative in his introduction to *Orot HaKodesh*:

> In the early morning I heard the sound of steps. Then the morning blessings, and the prayer of the *Akeidah*, in sublime song and melody. *"From the eternal heavens on high, remember the love of our ancestors..."*
>
> I listened; and I became a new person. Immediately I wrote, announcing that I had found more than I had hoped for. I had found for myself a Rav.

THE LONDON BOMB SHELTER

In late 1915, Rav Kook was invited to fill the rabbinic post at the Spitalfields Great Synagogue, known as "Mahzikei HaDath," in London. Rav Kook agreed to accept the position, but on one condition: that after the war, he would be free to return unhindered to Eretz Yisrael.

His private secretary, Rabbi Shimon Glitzenstein, recorded his experiences with Rav Kook during that time period in a booklet titled "Mazkir HaRav" ("The Rabbi's Secretary"). Glitzenstein included in the booklet the following account of a sleepless night he spent in a London bomb shelter together with the Rav.

During the aerial bombardment of London during the First World War,[7] the residents of the city took refuge in various shelters. The Jews who lived in the vicinity of Rav Kook took shelter in the cellar of the Mahzikei HaDath synagogue. Against his will, Rav Kook would also go there, but only to alleviate the fears of his family.

The cellar was crowded and suffocating. The children wailed, and the young people complained. Some of the men gathered around Rav Kook and began reciting *Tehillim* (Psalms) together. But as the noise and the sound of explosions increased, they stopped. Those musically inclined began to sing loudly in order to drown out the terrifying sounds from outside. Some people protested against the singing, but the rabbi encouraged the singers to raise their voices even louder.

---

[7] The first aerial bombardment of civilians in history took place on January 19, 1915, when German Zeppelins dropped 24 high-explosive bombs over several English towns. Over the next three years, the Germans dropped 5,800 bombs over England, killing 557 people and injuring over a thousand others (*Wikipedia*, "Aerial bombing of cities").

After several long hours, most had fallen asleep. Only Rav Kook remained calmly in his spot, with no sign of fatigue or distress. In his hand he held his small Bible. He recited chapter 43 of the Book of Psalms, which opens with the request, *"Grant me justice, O God. Take up my case against a merciless nation!"*

I was accustomed to the sound of the rabbi's recital of Psalms when he was alone in his room. He would read them loudly, with bitter weeping and an outpouring of the soul. But this recital of Psalms was different. I did not listen to the words, which he recited quietly, but to the unique melody which accompanied them. The tune was full of soul; it was permeated with a spiritual sweetness.

From the depth of his soul, Rav Kook poured forth his petitions before his Father in heaven. It was as if, through his voice, the entire Jewish nation was pleading, asking God for compassion and redemption. *"Send forth Your light and Your truth; they will guide me. They will bring me to Your holy mountain and to Your dwelling place"* (Psalms 43:3).

The rabbi was completely focused on his recitation. Even when it was announced that the danger had passed, he remained oblivious to the commotion of the people leaving the shelter. He continued reciting the chapter, in that soft, sweet melody, to its final verse.

THE BALFOUR DECLARATION

Rav Kook's secretary, Rabbi Shimon Glitzenstein, noted in his memoirs: "Not many days passed [after Rav Kook's arrival in London] when already his influence on all circles of Jewish life in this large and important community was felt. All recognized his extraordinary concern for the entire Jewish people."

Rav Kook certainly did not plan to spend three and a half years in London. But he would later describe the momentous events of this period – events in which he took an active role – as a "revelation of the hand of God."

Soon after his arrival, Rav Kook was forced to battle Jews who were working to undermine the Jewish people's hopes of national rebirth in the Land of Israel. Certain assimilated leaders of the British Jewish community, who considered themselves "Englishmen of the Mosaic faith," openly opposed the Zionist front. Due to their socio-economic and political standing, this powerful group, which included the staunchly anti-Zionist Lord Montagu, had great influence on the British government. They publicly declared to the British government that the Jewish religion has no connection to nationalism, and that they opposed all plans to designate Palestine as the Jewish homeland.

In a public notice titled, "In response to this national treachery," Rav Kook harshly condemned all those "who tear apart the Jewish soul" and shatter the wondrous unity of the Jewish religion and Jewish nationalism.

> The entire debate whether it is our national or our religious heritage that preserves and sustains us [as Jews] is a bitter mockery. The perfection of "*You are one*

and Your Name is one, and who is like Your nation, Israel, one nation in the land" is indivisible.

Rav Kook's public notice described the cruel injustices perpetrated by the nations over the centuries, and demanded that they atone for their terrible crimes by returning *Eretz Yisrael* to the Jewish people and assist in establishing an independent Jewish state. The letter was read in all British synagogues after the Sabbath Torah reading and made a deep impression. Rav Kook sent an additional letter urging the members of all British synagogues to immediately request that the British government "aid us in our demand to return to our holy land, as our eternal national home."

These efforts succeeded, and the damaging letter written by the influential Jewish leaders was disregarded. The major British newspapers noted the spontaneous protest, thus repairing the negative impression the assimilationists had created.

During the parliamentary debates over whether or not to authorize a national Jewish home in Palestine, several parliament members raised the claims advanced by the Jewish assimilationists. Such a mandate, they insisted, is contrary to the very spirit of Judaism.

Then Mr. James Kiley, a proponent of the idea of a Jewish home in Palestine, stood up and asked, "Upon whom shall we rely to decide the *religious* aspect of this issue – upon Lord Montagu, or upon Rabbi Kook, the rabbi of Mahzikei HaDath?"

After the Balfour Declaration was passed in 1917, the Jewish leaders held a large celebratory banquet in London, to which they invited lords, dignitaries, and members of Parliament. In speech after speech, Jewish communal and Zionist leaders thanked the British for their historic act.

When Rav Kook was honored with addressing the assembly, he announced:

> I have come not only to thank the British nation, but even more, to *congratulate* it for the privilege of making

48

this declaration. The Jewish nation is the "scholar" among the nations, the "people of the Book," and a nation of prophets. It is a great honor for any nation to come to its aid. I bless the British nation for having extended such honorable aid to the people of the Torah, so that they may return to their land and renew their homeland.

Lord Arthur Balfour and the Declaration (Wikimedia Commons)

Jerusalem

1919-1935

Rav Kook, 1924 (Wikimedia Commons)

"WHO ARE YOU, GREAT MOUNTAIN?"

In the summer of 1923, the Jewish community held a celebratory service in the country's most important synagogue, the Rabbi Yehudah Hasid Synagogue in Jerusalem's Old City.[8] The country had recently come under the rule of the British Mandate, and community leaders organized an assembly of prayers and thanks to the British government, in honor of King George V's birthday.

The general atmosphere in the country, however, was one of disappointment, even bitterness. The 1917 Balfour Declaration and the 1920 San Remo Conference had promised to establish a Jewish national home in Palestine. But in practice, the policies of the British Mandate told a different story. In an attempt to appease the Arabs, the

---

[8] Also known as the Hurva synagogue, it was founded in the early 1700s by followers of Rabbi Yehudah HeHasid. However, unexpected building costs, taxes, and bribes to Ottoman officials forced the founders into severe debt. In 1720, Arab lenders lost patience and burnt down the uncompleted synagogue. The building remained in ruins for well over a century, thus acquiring the name "Hurva" (destroyed) synagogue.

The synagogue was finally rebuilt in the 1850s. The construction was supervised by the sultan's official architect in a stately neo-Byzantine style, capped by a huge dome. One of the tallest structures in the Old City, visitors described it as "the glory of the Old City" and "most striking edifice in all of Palestine."

During the battle for the Old City in 1948, the synagogue was breached and damaged by the Jordanian Legion. Together with other synagogues in the Old City, the Hurva was systematically destroyed by the Jordanians soon after their occupation of the Old City in 1948. Reconstruction of the synagogue began after the area was liberated in the Six-Day War, and was completed in 2010.

British White Paper of 1922 placed severe limits on Jewish immigration. Britain furthermore split Mandatory Palestine into two, excluding all lands east of the Jordan River from Jewish settlement.

Rav Kook, now the Chief Rabbi of *Eretz Yisrael*, was one of the speakers at the 1923 assembly. The rabbi had returned to the country in 1919, accepting the post of Chief Rabbi of Jerusalem. His inauguration as Chief Rabbi of *Eretz Yisrael* had taken place in 1921, in the Rabbi Yehudah Hasid Synagogue.

In order to raise the spirits of the Jews of *Eretz Yisrael* – and to remind the British government of its promises to the Jewish people – Rav Kook chose to quote from that week's *Haftarah* reading, taken from the book of Zechariah. The reading was particularly appropriate: the prophet Zechariah had lived during the time of a previous return to Zion, when the Jewish people returned from the Babylonian exile some 2,500 years ago.

There are many parallels, Rav Kook noted, between that era and our own. The Jews returning from Babylonia were disillusioned and downhearted. And the foreign peoples whom the Babylonians had settled in the Land of Israel created many difficulties. Zechariah sought to reassure the discouraged Jewish settlers, calling out:

> *Who are you, great mountain? Before Zerubavel, you will be a flat plain!* (4:7)

To what "great mountain" was the prophet speaking?

The path leading toward the fulfillment of God's promise to His people, their return to Zion, was endorsed by the mighty empire of those days: Persia. Cyrus, the king of Persia, had officially appointed Zerubavel to oversee the rebuilding of the Jewish community in the Land of Israel. Zerubavel, a direct descendant of King Jehoiachin, the penultimate king of Judah, led the first band of Jews back to Jerusalem.

There were, however, many obstacles on the way. The prophet poetically refers to these hurdles as "great mountains," as they raised major difficulties and challenges and obstructed the return of the

54

Jewish people to Zion. And yet, Zechariah promised, before the king's representative, Zerubavel, these difficulties are nothing; he will flatten them like a level plain.

Rav Kook concluded his address, telling the people gathered in the synagogue: We live in similar times. God is fulfilling His promise to restore the Jewish people to their homeland. This time, it is through the mighty empire of Great Britain. It is our expectation that, in accordance with the declaration of His Majesty's government, the king's representative – Rav Kook was hinting to the British High Commissioner – will expedite the return of Israel to the Holy Land, despite the many difficulties obstructing this historic process.

"Who are you, great mountain?" Regardless of the complexity of the problems, despite the efforts of other nations to hinder and obstruct, before the powerful tool of Divine Providence, all of these obstacles will be smoothed over, and the path to redemption will become like "a level plain."

The magnificent dome of the Hurva Synagogue dominating the Jerusalem skyline, before 1899 (Wikimedia Commons)

PLANTING A TREE IN MAGDIEL

"At every possible occasion," wrote Rabbi Ze'ev Gold, "I tell the story of the remarkable lesson I was privileged to learn from our great master, the *gaon* and holy Rav Kook, may the memory of the righteous be a blessing."

Rabbi Gold (1889-1956), a leader of the religious-Zionist Mizrahi movement, once accompanied the Chief Rabbi to the community of Magdiel[9] in the Sharon area. The rabbis were invited to plant saplings in an official ceremony to inaugurate a new forest.

---

[9] The town of Magdiel was founded in 1924. Rav Kook objected to the name Magdiel, as this was the name of an Edomite chieftain (Gen. 36:43). Even worse, ancient Jewish tradition identifies Magdiel as Rome, the nation which conquered the Land of Israel and destroyed the Second Temple (see Rashi ad loc, from *Pirkei d'Rabbi Eliezer*). This did not, however, prevent Rav Kook's participation in the tree-planting ceremony in the town.

It was rumored that Rav Kook had predicted that the name Magdiel would not last. And in fact, in 1964, the town of Magdiel was combined with its neighboring towns, and the new municipality was renamed "Hod Hasharon."

Rabbi Tzvi Yehudah Kook related that, soon after this event, he received a letter from a resident of Netanya. For many years, the author of the letter had studied his father's books, which he found very inspiring. But when he heard a rumor that Rav Kook predicted the neighboring town of Magdiel would "be erased from the map," he found this so disturbing that he stopped studying the rabbi's writings.

Following the 1964 municipality change, the Netanya resident offered his apologies. He now understood how Rav Kook's prediction was fulfilled, as only the *name* Magdiel was erased from the map, with Hod Hasharon taking its place. He expressed his sincere regrets, promising to once again study the Rav's writings.

As Rav Kook was handed a sampling to plant, Rabbi Gold was amazed to see the rabbi's reaction. His face shone like a burning torch, and his entire body quivered with excitement. He did not use the hoe he had been provided, but knelt down to the soil and dug a hole in the earth with his bare hands. Hands shaking, he reverently placed the sampling in the ground, while murmuring his gratitude to God for the privilege of planting a tree in the Holy Land.

On the trip back to Jerusalem, Rabbi Gold turned to the Chief Rabbi. "Why did you exhibit such deep emotions when you planted a tree into the ground? Nowadays, thank God, hundreds of trees are planted every day in the Land of Israel!"

"As I held that young sapling in my hands," Rav Kook replied, "I remembered how the Sages elucidated the verse, '*Follow the Eternal your God... and cling to Him*' (Deuteronomy 13:5). They asked:

> Is it possible for flesh and blood to ascend to the heavens and cling to the Shechinah, about Whom it is written, "*For the Eternal your God is a consuming fire*" (Deuteronomy 4:24)?
>
> Rather, understand the verse as follows: At the beginning of creation, the Holy One engaged in planting, as it says, "*God planted a garden in Eden*" (Gen. 2:8). Similarly, when you enter in the Land of Israel, you should first engage in planting, as it is written, "*When you will come into the Land, you shall plant all types of fruit trees*" (Leviticus 19:23). (*Vayikra Rabbah* 25:3)

"When I grasped that tender sapling in my hands and prepared to plant it in the holy earth," Rav Kook continued, "I contemplated these words of the Sages. I felt as if, at that very moment, I was clinging to the Shechinah, and I was overwhelmed with feelings of awe and reverence!"

BLASTS THAT PENETRATE THE HEART

In a quiet Jerusalem neighborhood, the peaceful autumn air of Rosh Hashanah morning was shattered by the jarring noise of construction, with hammers pounding and saws rattling. The neighbors were furious at this blatant desecration of the High Holidays – and in the holy city of Jerusalem! One neighbor yelled at the workmen, but the young men shrugged and continued their labors. They needed to finish this building as soon as possible, even if it meant working on the Rosh Hashanah holiday.

Angry and frustrated, the neighbors sent an urgent message to the Chief Rabbi. Surely he would put a stop to this public desecration of the holiday.

Soon after, a messenger from Rav Kook arrived at the construction site. Shofar in hand, he surprised the workers by greeting them with warm New Year's wishes.

Shofar blowing, Matson Collection, ca. 1934-1939 (LOC)

He then announced that the Chief Rabbi had sent him to blow the shofar for them, in accordance with the obligation to hear the shofar on Rosh Hashanah. He respectfully asked them to take a break from their work and listen to the shofar blasts. The messenger proceeded to recite the traditional blessing over the shofar and began to blow.

The gentle message from Rav Kook, together with the sounds of the shofar,

58

achieved their goal. Each blast shook the delicate chords in the hearts of the young workers, awakening the Jewish spark in their souls. They laid down their work tools and gathered around the man blowing the shofar. Some were so moved that their eyes filled with tears. The ancient blasts of the shofar, reverberating in the unfinished building, transported them back to their childhood homes. They saw images of their grandfathers, the shtetl and the synagogue, a world of Jews standing together in prayer on Rosh Hashanah.

Questions began to pour out, one after another. What happened to us? Where are we? What have we come to? The young men stood around the emissary, confused and absorbed in thought.

When the shofar blowing was over, there was no need for words. Unanimously, the workers decided to stop working. Some asked the messenger if they could accompany him. They quickly changed their clothes and joined in the holiday prayers at Rav Kook's yeshiva.

* * *

In a letter from that time, Rav Kook described his approach on how to reach out to the non-religious:

> A friendly word is effective; an expression of comradeship and respect will bring others close. We should not abandon the good and straight path that is illuminated with love and goodwill, peace and friendship. We must break down the wall that divides brothers, and speak heart to heart, soul to soul.
>
> Then our words will certainly be heard. And these sons of ours will suddenly raise themselves up. They will crown their powerful aspiration to build the land and the nation with the eternal ideals of lofty holiness.

THE POEL MIZRAHI KITCHEN

Things were not looking good for Abraham Mavrach. It was already the first of the month of Av, and the clerk would not let him see the Chief Rabbi and present his urgent question. The rabbis were in an important meeting, the secretary explained, and could not be disturbed.

Mr. Mavrach was a founding member of the Poel Mizrahi, an organization established in 1922 to meet the needs of religious pioneers in *Eretz Yisrael*. One of the most important decisions made during the first assembly of the Poel Mizrahi was to open kosher kitchens for new immigrants and workers. This was a vital need, since the religious workers could not eat in the Histadrut kitchens where non-kosher food was served and the sanctity of the Sabbath was not honored.

Mavrach described the situation in the *Hatzofeh* newspaper:

> The religious pioneers suffered greatly. They could not afford to eat in a restaurant and enjoy a hot meal, and on the Sabbath they missed the Jewish milieu and an atmosphere of holiness. Therefore we established the kitchens of the Poel Mizrahi to provide the religious workers with inexpensive and tasty meals, and also to serve as a social center. The workers would read, hold meetings, discuss, and attend classes and lectures. They organized Torah classes in the evenings, and they would dance on joyous occasions. The kitchens were filled with singing. Especially on the Sabbath and the holidays, they sang the *zemirot* with holy yearnings and

60

deep emotion. It is not surprising that the kosher kitchens also attracted many non-religious workers.

Although the food was sold at cost, not all of the diners could afford to eat everything on the limited menu. However, the meat portions and soups were a necessary staple for the hungry manual laborers.

It was due to those meat meals that a thorny problem came up. During the Nine Days of Av, Jewish law prohibits eating meat due to national mourning for the destruction of the Temple.[10] The administrators of the Jerusalem branch of the Poel Mizrahi met to find an alternative for the meat meals, especially for the manual laborers, but failed to come up with an appropriate substitute.

Some of the Poel Mizrahi members despaired of finding a workable solution. "Why should we assume responsibility for this?" Lacking a better alternative, they proposed that the kitchen be closed down for the duration of the Nine Days.

One member, however, refused to give up: Abraham Mavrach. He suggested turning to the Chief Rabbinate. Perhaps the rabbis would find a leniency that would permit the new customers to eat meat so that they would not go back to eating in the non-kosher kitchens.

The other members laughed at this suggestion. "Do you really think that the Rabbinate will agree to the slaughter of sheep and oxen during the Nine Days in the holy city of Jerusalem?"

In fact, no one was even willing to accompany him to the Chief Rabbinate. So, on the first of Av, Mavrach went alone. And when he arrived, the clerk refused to let him interrupt the meeting and speak with the rabbis.

Mavrach persevered. "This is an urgent question," he explained. "I come as a representative of the Poel Mizrahi."

---

[10] Both the First Temple of King Solomon and the Second Temple were destroyed on the same date – the ninth day of Av.

At his insistence, Rabbi Samuel Weber, chief secretary of the Rabbinate, left the meeting and listened to the problem. The rabbi suggested arranging for a Talmudic tractate to be completed every day, and then serving meat at the *se'udat mitzvah*, a meal celebrating the fulfillment of a mitzvah. But Mavrach explained that such an arrangement would be nearly impossible to implement.

Rabbi Weber then disappeared into the Rabbinate chambers. After a few minutes, he beckoned the visitor to follow him.

As he entered, Mavrach spied Rav Kook at the head of the table. Sephardic Chief Rabbi Yaakov Meir sat to his right, and other prominent rabbis were seated around the table. Rav Kook requested that the visitor to approach the table.

Mavrach stood before the rabbis and presented the problem of the kitchen during the Nine Days. He described the great benefit it provided to the members of the Poel Mizrahi and the workers who remained faithful to their Jewish heritage.

"I am aware of the importance of the kitchen," Rav Kook replied. He then sank into deep thought. The other rabbis waited in silence for Rav Kook's decision.

Rav Kook turned to the guest. "Do you think that some of the workers who eat there will end up going to a non-kosher kitchen?"

"Certainly," he responded. "They ate there beforehand."

"If that is the case," Rav Kook pronounced, "your kitchen is serving a *se'udat mitzvah*. 'Let the humble eat and be satisfied' (Psalms 27:22)."

Astounded, Mavrach remained frozen to his spot. Rav Kook smiled kindly. "Do you have another question?"

Mavrach replied that he was uncertain about the Rav's decision. Did this mean that *everyone* could eat meat there? Rav Kook repeated his words, and explained that everyone – even those who would not be tempted to eat at a non-kosher kitchen – could eat meat in the kitchen, because it would be serving a *se'udat mitzvah*.

Despite his amazement, Mavrach managed to steal a glance at the other rabbis in the room. It seemed to him that they were also surprised by the rabbi's decision, but they raised no objections.

Se'udat Mitzvah for All

Noted author Rabbi Tzvi Kaplan penned an article analyzing this unusual Halakhic decision at length. For those workers who would have eaten in the non-kosher kitchen, it is clearly preferable that they disregard the custom of not eating meat during the Nine Days rather than violate the Biblical stricture on eating non-kosher food. But how could Rav Kook permit meat to those who would *not* have eaten non-kosher food?

Rabbi Kaplan noted that at a *se'udat mitzvah* during the Nine Days (such as at a *brit milah* or when completing a tractate of Talmud), permission to eat meat is granted not only for those performing the mitzvah, but for all who are present. Every Jew is responsible for his fellow Jew, and that includes making sure that he eats kosher food. A meal which accomplishes this goal certainly qualifies as a *se'udat mitzvah*. The simple meals provided by the Poel Mizrahi kitchen in those years saved many Jews from eating non-kosher meals. Rav Kook was therefore able to permit all present to eat, since, as he reasoned, "your kitchen is serving a *se'udat mitzvah*."

Jewish workers in Tel Aviv, 1909

THE YEMENITE LABORER'S DREAM

This remarkable story was told by Mr. Yigal Gal-Ezer, who served as Israel's vice state comptroller. In his younger days, Gal-Ezer would often visit Rav Kook's home in order to be inspired by his holy presence.

During one of my visits, I found the rabbi in his study, absorbed in a complex Talmudic topic. Suddenly I heard a hesitant knocking at the door. The door opened partially, and a Yemenite Jew – slight of stature, with streaks of white in his beard and long peiyot– entered the room.

The guest closed the door behind him and stood in the doorway, his back to the door. He lowered his head to the floor, afraid to look at the rabbi directly.

Rav Kook raised his eyes from his Talmud and looked at the man kindly. "Come closer, my son." With a gentle voice, the rabbi tried to instill confidence in the visitor.

With slow steps, the man drew near to the rabbi's desk. He remained standing, head down.

"What is disturbing you, my son?"

"Honored rabbi," the Yemenite said. "I came to ask the rabbi an important question."

"Ask, my son, ask."

"For twenty-five years, I have performed backbreaking labor, from morning to evening. I weeded plots of land so that orchards could be planted. I planted saplings, dug up stones from fields, excavated foundations for buildings in *Eretz Yisrael*. I spent all my strength in

64

exhausting manual labor. And yet I barely earn enough to support my family."

Embarrassed, the Yemenite lowered his voice. "I would like to ask: is it permissible for me to immigrate to America? Perhaps there my fortune will shine and I will be able to properly support my family...."

The visitor finished his short speech and remained standing in silence.

For several minutes, Rav Kook sat, deep in thought. Abruptly, he stood up, pointed to his chair and commanded the man, "Sit."

The visitor became filled with trepidation. "Honored Rabbi," he stammered. "It is improper that a stranger should sit on your chair."

"Sit," the rabbi repeated.

With short, reluctant steps, the Yemenite walked around the desk until he came to the rabbi's chair. He slowly lowered himself into the seat.

As soon as he sat down, his head dropped to the desk and he fell into a deep sleep. A short while later, he woke, startled.

"What happened when you slept?" asked the Rav.

"I dreamt that I had passed on to the next world," he reported. "My soul ascended to heaven. When I reached heaven's gates, there was an angel standing at the entrance who directed me to the heavenly court. There I saw scales – scales of justice."

The Yemenite laborer continued his account. "Suddenly, carriages drawn by horses rushed in front of me. The carriages were loaded with packages. Some of the packages were small, some were medium-sized, and some were large. The angels began unloading the packages, and they placed them on one side of the scales. That side of the scales plunged downwards due to the weight, until it nearly reached the ground.

"'What is the meaning of these packages?' I asked the angel standing before me.

"'These, o mortal, are your sins and faults from your days on earth. *Everything* is accounted for,' he replied. My spirits fell.

"Then other carriages arrived. These carriages were loaded with dirt, rocks, stones, and sand. As the angels loaded them on the other side of the scales, it began to lift up – slightly – the side of sins and transgressions.

"'What is the meaning of these bundles of dirt?' I asked.

"'These are the stones, rocks, and dirt which your hands labored to remove from the ground of the Holy Land. They have come to speak in your defense, for your part in the mitzvah of *yishuv ha'aretz*, settling the Land of Israel.'

Yemenite construction worker cutting stones in Jerusalem, 1922.

"Trembling, I stared at the side of merits. I saw it dipping lower and lower, lifting the opposite side. Finally the side of merits ceased moving. It stopped as it outweighed the sins – but just barely."

"You see, my son," Rav Kook told the man gently. "You have received your answer from heaven."

RAV KOOK AND HEBRON

A somber gathering assembled in Jerusalem's Yeshurun synagogue. The large synagogue and its plaza were packed as crowds attended a memorial service for the Jews of Hebron who had been killed during the Arab riots six months earlier, on August 24th, 1929.

On that tragic Sabbath day, news of deadly rioting in Hebron reached the Jewish leaders in Jerusalem. Yitzchak Ben-Zvi, then director of the National Committee, hurried to Rav Kook's house. Together they hastened to meet with Harry Luke, the acting British high commissioner, to urge him to take action and protect the Jews of Hebron.

The Chief Rabbi demanded that the British take severe and immediate measures against the Arab rioters.

"What can be done?" Luke asked.

Rav Kook's response was to the point. "Shoot the murderers!"

"But I have received no such orders."

"Then *I* am commanding you!" Rav Kook roared. "In the name of humanity's moral conscience, I demand this!"

Rav Kook held the acting commissioner responsible for British inaction during the subsequent massacre. Not long after this heated exchange, an official reception was held in Jerusalem, and Mr. Luke held out his hand to greet the Chief Rabbi. To the shock of many, Rav Kook refused to shake it.

With quiet fury, the rabbi explained, "I do not shake hands defiled with Jewish blood."

Funeral for a victim of 1929 Hebron massacre

The day after the rioting in Hebron, the extent of the massacre was revealed. Arab mobs had slaughtered 67 Jews — yeshiva students, elderly rabbis, women, and children. The British police had done little to protect them. The Jewish community of Hebron was destroyed, and their property looted and stolen. The British shipped the survivors off to Jerusalem.

The *tzaddik* Rabbi Arieh Levine accompanied Rav Kook that Sunday to Hadassah Hospital on HaNevi'im Street in order to hear news of the Hebron community by telephone. Rabbi Levine recalled the frightful memories that would be forever etched in his heart.

When the Rav heard about the murder of the holy martyrs, he fell backwards and fainted. After coming to, he cried bitterly and tore his clothes "over the house of Israel and God's people who have fallen by the sword." He sat in the dust and recited the blessing, *"Baruch Dayan Ha'Emet"* ("Blessed is the True Judge").

For some time after that, his bread was the bread of tears and he slept without a pillow. Old age suddenly befell him, and he began to suffer terrible pains. This tragedy brought about the illness from which the Rav never recovered.

The Memorial Service

Six months after the massacre, grieving crowds filled the Yeshurun synagogue in Jerusalem. A mourning atmosphere, like that on the fast of Tisha B'Av, lingered in the air as they assembled in pained silence. Survivors of the massacre, who had witnessed the atrocities before their eyes, recited *Kaddish* for family members murdered in the rioting.

Rabbi Jacob Joseph Slonim, who had lost his son (a member of the Hebron municipal council) and grandchildren in the massacre, opened the assembly in the name of the remnant of the Hebron community.

"No healing has taken place during the past six months," he reported. "The murder and the theft have not been rectified. The British government and the Jewish leadership have done nothing to correct the situation. They have not worked to reclaim Jewish property and resettle Hebron."

Afterwards, the Chief Rabbi rose to speak:

> The holy martyrs of Hebron do not need a memorial service. The Jewish people can never forget the holy and pure souls who were slaughtered by murderers and vile thugs.
>
> Rather, we must remember and remind the Jewish people not to forget the city of the Patriarchs. The people must know what Hebron means to us.
>
> We have an ancient tradition that "The actions of the fathers are signposts for their descendants." When the weak-hearted spies arrived at Hebron, they were frightened by the fierce nations who lived in the land. But *"Caleb quieted the people for Moses. He said, 'We must go forth and conquer the land. We can do it!'"* (Numbers 13:30)
>
> Despite the terrible tragedy that took place in Hebron, we announce to the world, "Our strength is now like our strength was then." We will not abandon our holy places and sacred aspirations. Hebron is the

69

city of our fathers, the city of the Machpeilah cave where our Patriarchs are buried. It is the city of David, the cradle of our sovereign monarchy.

Those who discourage the ones trying to rebuild the Jewish community in Hebron with arguments of political expedience; those who scorn and say, "What are those wretched Jews doing?"; those who refuse to help rebuild Hebron – they are attacking the very roots of our people. In the future, they will have to give account for their actions. If ruffians and hooligans have repaid our kindness with malice, we have only one eternal response: Jewish Hebron will once again be built, in honor and glory!

The inner meaning of Hebron is to draw strength and galvanize ourselves with the power of *Netzach Yisrael*, Eternal Israel.

Desecrated synagogue in Hebron, 1929 (Wikimedia Commons)

That proud Jew, Caleb, announced years later, "*I am still strong... As my strength was then, so is my strength now*" (Joshua 14:11). We, too, announce to the world: our strength now is as our strength was then. We shall reestablish Hebron in even greater glory, with peace and security for every Jew. With God's help, we will merit to see Hebron completely rebuilt, speedily in our days.

THE KOTEL AFFAIR

Rabbi Zvi Yehudah Kook recalled the tremendous pressures placed upon his father that evening in the Kiryat Moshe neighborhood of Jerusalem. He wrote:

> How intense, how grave, how dire were the warnings and intimidations at that time, with all of their menacing threats. Two nations [the Arabs and the British] were goading us with lies and murderous traps, to sign an agreement and relinquish [Jewish] ownership over the Kotel, the remaining wall of our Holy Temple.

During the tenure of the first British High Commissioner, Hajj Amin al-Husseini was appointed Mufti of Jerusalem, the spiritual and national leader of the Arabs. One of the many devices that al-Husseini employed in his fight against the Jewish return to *Eretz Yisrael* was to repudiate all Jewish rights to the *Kotel HaMa'aravi*, the Western Wall.[11]

---

[11] Rav Tzvi Yehudah later published an article entitled "*Behind Our Wall*," analyzing the significance of the Kotel for the Jewish people:

> Even if the disgrace of ruin hides its beauty, and prominent marks of destruction and clouds of desolation cast shadows over its radiance; even if it is hidden behind a thicket of dark and squalid alleys, as it is shoved aside in the cruelty of its neighbors, surrounding it from all sides, trying to overrun its borders, to subdue and consume its legacy. Nonetheless, like a stone fortress, it stands guard, without moving and

The Arabs gained a partial victory in 1922, when the British Mandatory Government issued a ban against placing benches near the Kotel. In 1928, British officers interrupted the Yom Kippur service and forcibly dismantled the *mehitzah* separating men and women during prayer.

A few months later, the Mufti and his cohorts devised a new provocation. They began holding Muslim religious ceremonies opposite the Kotel, precisely when the Jews were praying. To make matters worse, the British authorities granted the Arabs permission to transform the building adjacent to the Kotel into a mosque, complete with a tower for the muezzin, the crier calling Moslems to prayer five times a day. The muezzin's vociferous trills were certain to disturb the Jewish prayers.

Active Arab turbulence reached its peak during the bloody riots of 1929. On the Tenth of Av, thousands of Arabs swarmed the Kotel,

---

without allowing its inner nobility to be sullied. It remains pure and lofty in the strength of its very essence...

For it is a remnant of the holy and precious, of the Divine abode. In the wonderful quality of its very survival, it bears witness to world events and millennia of human history.

There are hearts and there are hearts; there are human hearts, and there are hearts of stone.

There are stones and there are stones; there are mute stones, and there are stones which are hearts.

These stones, remnants of our dwelling on high, "retain their holiness even in desolation" (*Megillah* 3:3), for "God's Presence has never left the Western Wall" (*Tanhuma Shemot* 10).... *These stones are our hearts!*

We all know that this wall, despite its somber simplicity and signs of ruin and exile, is not a "Wailing Wall," as it is called by strangers and foreigners. For us, it is a wealth of life, a concealed treasure of light and strength, guarded and secured by our tears. (*LeNetivot Yisrael* vol. I, pp. 22-25).

chasing away the Jews praying there and burning several Torah scrolls. The following week, rioting broke out in Jerusalem and spread throughout the country. Nearly a hundred Jews were slaughtered in the riots, primarily in Hebron and Jerusalem.

In the summer of 1930, the League of Nations dispatched a committee to clarify the issue of ownership of the Western Wall. The Arabs claimed to be the rightful owners, not only of the Temple Mount but of the Kotel as well. They rejected any agreement that permitted Jews to pray at the Kotel. It is solely a Muslim site, the Mufti claimed; the Jews may pray at the Kotel only by the good grace of the Arabs.

"British police at the Wailing Wall" by Verlag Wien, 1934. (Wikimedia Commons)

When Rav Kook appeared before the commission, he turned to the chairman with indignation: "What do you mean when you declare, 'The commission will decide to whom the Wall belongs'? Does this commission or the League of Nations own the Wall? Who gave you permission to decide to whom it belongs?"

The Chief Rabbi then quoted Rashi's commentary to the first verse in Genesis: "The entire world belongs to the Creator… and He transferred ownership of the entire Land of Israel" – *including the Kotel*, Rav Kook added – "to the Jewish people." With a sharp look at the commission members, he emphasized, "No power in the world, not the League of Nations, nor this commission, can take away this God-given right from us."

The chairman retorted that the Jews have not been in control of the Land of Israel or the Wall for close to two thousand years.

At this point, Rav Kook decided the members of the commission needed to learn a lesson in Jewish law. Calmly and respectfully, he explained: "In Jewish law, the concept of *yei'ush be'alim* – despair of the owner – applies also to real estate. [That is, the owner of a stolen tract of land forfeits his ownership if he gives up hope of ever retrieving it.] But if a person's land is stolen and he continuously protests the theft, the owner retains his ownership for all time."[12]

Rav Kook's proud appearance before the commission made a profound impact on the Jewish community. The *Hator* newspaper commented:

> We cannot refrain from mentioning once again the Chief Rabbi of *Eretz Yisrael*, who sanctified God and Israel with his testimony. The witnesses who preceded him stood meekly, with tottering knees. After the Chief Rabbi's appearance, we felt a bit relieved, as if a weight had been lifted from our hearts. He raised our heads, straightened our spines, and restored dignity to the Torah and our nation.

The British Mandatory government suggested a compromise, according to which the Jews would recognize Arab ownership of the

---

[12] Whether land can be stolen is a subject of disagreement between Maimonides and Rabbeinu Asher. The *Shulchan Aruch (Choshen Mishpat* 371:1) rules like Maimonides, that land can never be stolen. Later authorities qualify this ruling and write that there are situations when land can be stolen, such as when the owner fears for his life if he does not relinquish his land (*Aruch HaShulchan* ad loc).

With regard to the Land of Israel, there was never *yei'ush be'alim*, as the Jewish people continually protested the theft of their homeland in their daily prayers for the return of Jerusalem and Zion.

Kotel, and the Arabs in return would permit Jews to approach the Wall. (The right for Jews *to pray* at the Kotel, however, was not explicitly included in the proposed agreement.)

Due to the tense political situation – particularly in light of the murderous Arab rioting the previous year – the Va'ad Leumi (the executive committee of the Jewish National Assembly) was prepared to recognize Arab ownership of the Kotel. However, the Va'ad Leumi stipulated that the Arabs must explicitly recognize the right of Jews to pray there.

Because this was a religious matter, the Mandatory government required that the Va'ad Leumi's proposal be approved by the religious authority of the Jews, namely, the Rabbinate. In order to apply greater pressure on the rabbis, the Va'ad Leumi sent delegations simultaneously to the two Chief Rabbis, Rav Kook and Rabbi Yaakov Meir, as well as to Rabbi Yosef Chaim Zonnenfeld, who represented Agudath Israel.[13]

A delegation from the Va'ad, headed by Yitzchak Ben-Zvi, visited Rav Kook and tried to persuade him to approve the plan. It is a matter of life and death, they argued; only by renouncing Jewish ownership will we assuage the Arabs and bring peace to Israel.

Despite intense pressure from the Va'ad Leumi, Rav Kook refused to authorize the proposal. "The Chief Rabbinate has no authority to do such a thing," he explained. "The Jewish people did not empower us to surrender the Western Wall on its behalf. Our ownership of the Kotel is Divine in nature; and it is by virtue of this ownership that we come to pray at the Kotel."

The rabbi cautioned the delegation, "I cannot relinquish that which God gave to the Jewish people. If, Heaven forbid, we surrender the Kotel, God may not wish to return it to us!"

---

[13] Agudath Israel was established in 1912 as the umbrella organization of Haredi (ultra-orthodox) Jews who opposed the Zionist movement. Rejecting the Chief Rabbinate of *Eretz Yisrael* due to its ties to Zionist organizations, Agudath Israel appointed Rabbi Zonnenfeld as its spiritual leader.

As it turned out, the Arabs refused even to consider granting the right of Jewish prayer at the Kotel, and the proposal died. Indeed, after the War of Independence, although the cease-fire agreement provided for the right of Jews to approach the Kotel, the Jordanians ignored this provision. Only nineteen years later, when the Kotel was restored to its rightful owners in the Six-Day War, were the Jewish people once again able to pray unhindered at the Western Wall.[14]

---

[14] Menachem Porush, chairman of Agudath Israel, contributed the following detail regarding this incident:

When Rav Kook received the proposal, he stated that he would not agree to relinquish the Jewish claim to the Kotel under any circumstances. He also dispatched a personal messenger to Rabbi Zonnenfeld to inform him of his refusal, and to urge him not to show the British any lack of determination in the matter.

Rabbi Zonnenfeld, when he received notice of the proposal, also refused to agree. Afraid that Rav Kook might not be firm in refusing the proposal, Rabbi Zonnenfeld dispatched his own messenger to Rav Kook to inform him of his policy and to request that he not show any willingness to compromise on the matter.

The two messengers, who happened to be friends, chanced upon each other in the street and discussed their missions. Both were relieved when they realized that there was no need to deliver their respective messages. Thus, the plan, which would have compromised Jewish rights to the Kotel for generations, died aborning.

THE JERUSALEM POLICE OFFICER

Rav Kook was overjoyed with the good news: David Tidhar, a Jewish officer serving in the British Mandatory police force, had announced that he was engaged to be married. The rabbi insisted that the wedding be held in his own residence and that he would provide the wedding meal. Rav Kook even invited students from the yeshiva to join in the festivities.

Many people were surprised. Why was Rav Kook so fond of this particular policeman?

Rav Kook explained that David Tidhar had *zekhut avot* – ancestral merits. His father, Reb Moshe Betzalel Todrosovich, was a wealthy Jaffa philanthropist who had been instrumental in bringing Rav Kook to serve as rabbi of Jaffa. Reb Moshe Betzalel supported numerous religious projects in Jaffa, especially anything related to Jewish education and assisting those in need. This fine man, Rav Kook declared, is certainly deserving of our thanks and gratitude.

But Rav Kook's appreciation of David Tidhar was also based on his appreciation for the young man's own character and deeds. Their close ties took on greater importance when Tidhar became an officer in the Jerusalem police force. The Chief Rabbi would often turn to him for assistance in releasing a prisoner or to ameliorate a prisoner's conditions in jail.

On one unusual occasion, however, Rav Kook requested Tidhar's help in placing a man under arrest.

A certain resident of Jerusalem had decided to abandon his family, intending on leaving his wife without a proper divorce. Lacking an official bill of divorce (a *get*), the poor woman would become an *agunah*, trapped in her marriage and unable to remarry.

The scoundrel intended to flee Jerusalem on the early morning train. Legally, there was no way to stop him. The request to detain him had been submitted to the regional court, but the order could only be approved after the judge arrived at ten o'clock mid-morning.

Hearing of the situation, Rav Kook turned to Tidhar. The resourceful police officer came up with an unconventional

Jewish policemen on patrol in Jerusalem, 1936 (PikiWiki)

solution to deal with the case. He dispatched an undercover detective to the train station. The detective found an excuse to start a fight with the man. The altercation began with harsh words and quickly progressed to fisticuffs.

Policemen instantly appeared and arrested the two brawlers, hauling them in to the Me'ah She'arim police station. At that point, Tidhar arrived at the station. He detained the man until Rav Kook sent word that the court order had been obtained. He was then able to officially place the man under arrest.

In another incident, Tidhar sought to prevent the deportation of Jewish immigrants – a deportation that he himself had been detailed to carry out.

The British passport office sent Tidhar a long list of illegal immigrants. The list included many details: names, addresses, ages, and so on. Tidhar was astounded. How had the British obtained so much information about the immigrants?

The answer was not long in coming. British immigration officials had posed as Jewish aid workers, going from house to house in the

Jerusalem neighborhoods. Using this ploy, they tricked the immigrants into divulging their identifying details.

As police commander, Tidhar was the officer ordered to expel forty hapless families – on the day before Yom Kippur! It would have been a heart-breaking sight. Tidhar met with the Jewish city council. He requested that the refugees be provided with food and clothing, and he gave them a twelve-hour reprieve before executing the deportation.

The council's immigration department agreed. They provided for the immigrants' immediate needs and secretly transferred them to distant neighborhoods, thus forestalling the deportation orders.

In order to assist the refugees, Tidhar needed to work on Yom Kippur. Following Rav Kook's advice, he dressed as an Arab. This way, the Jewish immigrants would not be disturbed by the sight of a Jew desecrating the holiest day of the year – even if his labors were for their own benefit.

High Commissioner Herbert Samuel and Rav Kook in Jerusalem, 1925 (Wikimedia Commons)

"There are two men," Rav Kook would say, "who assist me in maintaining order in religious affairs in Jerusalem. The first is the British High Commissioner, Herbert Samuel. And the second is police officer David Tidhar."

"However, there is a difference between the two," the rabbi observed. "The commissioner always confers first with his legal advisor, so his assistance is often delayed. Officer Tidhar, on the other hand, is diligent and energetic. He does whatever he promises, quickly overcoming all obstacles."

David Tidhar admitted, "The British officers thought that they were my commanding officers. But my true commanding officer was Rav Kook. For me, any request of the rabbi was an order, which I tried to discharge to the best of my ability. I considered it a great privilege to fulfill the Chief Rabbi's wishes."

THE SECOND SEDER IN JERUSALEM

In the spring of 1934, many Jewish tourists from Europe and the United States traveled to *Eretz Yisrael* for the Passover holiday. Hundreds ascended to Jerusalem, excited to celebrate the festival in the holy city.

The Jewish National Fund, wishing to properly welcome these guests – and potential donors – decided to organize a Seder for them on the second day (*Yom Tov Sheini*) of Passover. In order to attract religious Jews, the JNF turned to the Chief Rabbi, requesting that he sponsor the event and supervise the kashruth of the festive meal.

Ordinarily, Rav Kook was only too happy to help the JNF and promote the redemption of land in *Eretz Yisrael*. On this occasion, however, he refused. He was not willing to take part in organizing a second Seder in Jerusalem. Observing the holiday for an additional day – that is for Jews residing in the Diaspora, he explained. We who live in the Land of Israel must protect the honor of *Eretz Yisrael*.

Why did Rav Kook oppose a public second Seder so vehemently?

Like many other Halakhic authorities in Jerusalem, he favored the opinion of the Hakham Tzvi,[15] who ruled that a tourist visiting in *Eretz Yisrael* should act like a local resident and observe only one day of *Yom Tov*. In practice, he would tell visitors from outside of Israel that they should recite the regular weekday prayers on the second day of *Yom Tov*, and observe *Yom Tov Sheini* only by avoiding forbidden work and not eating *hametz* (leavened bread) on the eighth day of Passover.

---

[15] Rabbi Tzvi Ashkenazi (1656-1718), rabbi of Amsterdam and author of widely respected responsa.

Yet this ruling was difficult for many religious Jews to accept. They were accustomed to attending the holiday services on the second day of *Yom Tov*. And the second Passover Seder was particularly important to them. How could they skip one year, knowing that the following festival they would once again be observing two days of *Yom Tov*?

Once a visiting rabbi from Pressburg arrived in Jerusalem and sought Rav Kook's counsel as to what he should do on the second day of *Yom Tov*.

When Rav Kook heard the question, he gave a pained look. "Most tourists don't even ask. And the few who do ask do not abide by my ruling. So why should I give a ruling?"

It was only after the visitor persisted, promising to follow the Chief Rabbi's decision, that Rav Kook gave his ruling, as described above.

Imagine, Rav Kook noted, if ten Jews from Israel were to walk into a synagogue in a city in the Diaspora on the second day of *Yom Tov* and publicly don tefillin and pray the weekday service. Would there not be a vociferous reaction?

The rule in such a case is that a Jew from Israel should pray the weekday prayers and don tefillin in private. Publicly, he should wear holiday clothes and outwardly observe the holiday.

Why then do the Jews of Diaspora fail to understand, even if they choose not to follow the ruling of the Hakham Tzvi, that the honor of *Eretz Yisrael* requires them to observe the second day of *Yom Tov* in private? Yet they insist on organizing public festival prayers on the second day – even at the Kotel!

Rav Kook's Condition

The JNF representatives, who realized that the Chief Rabbi's participation was critical for the success of their Seder, deliberated how to overcome his opposition to the plan. In the end they approached one of the older students in his yeshiva with the proposal that, for a very respectable fee, the student supervise the Seder. They stipulated, however, that he secure Rav Kook's approval for the event.

The young scholar, unaware of Rav Kook's previous refusal, happily accepted the proposition. The amount offered was sufficient to provide for his family's needs for several months. He hurried to the Rav to gain his approval.

Rav Kook now faced a difficult dilemma. Always sensitive to the needs of others, he knew how important this extra income was to the young scholar and his family. But what about the honor of *Eretz Yisrael*?

After considering the matter for a few moments, Rav Kook's face lit up. "Please tell the JNF," he replied, "that I too have a condition. If they are willing to accede, I will give my *hechsher* and authorize the event."

The rabbi continued: "My condition is that they invite the band of the Jerusalem Institute for the Blind to play music at the Seder. Any publicity for the JNF Seder must prominently advertise the band's participation."

"After all," he beamed, "everyone knows that musical instruments are not played on a Jewish holiday. A Passover Seder with a band playing in the background – that is not a real Seder!"

Rav Kook with American philanthropist Harry Fischel at the Chief Rabbi's home in Jerusalem in 1927.

THE FATAL MISTAKE

In the icy courtyard of the Israeli embassy in Warsaw, an old man stood alone, waiting. He was just bones, almost no flesh. His cheekbones protruded; his eyes had a deadened look. Despite the bitter cold of the Polish winter, his clothes were in tatters.

Baruch Duvdevani, who had studied at Rav Kook's Mercaz HaRav yeshiva as a young man, spent the winter of 1956 in Poland. Director of the Jewish Agency's Aliyah department, Duvdevani worked from morning to evening organizing the immigration of thousands of Polish Jews who had fled to Russia during World War II.

Duvdevani noticed the old man standing in the corner. He realized that the man was waiting for him to finish speaking with the other Polish Jews gathered at the embassy courtyard.

When the old man saw the opportunity, he approached Duvdevani.

"Are you from Jerusalem?" he asked.

"Yes, I am."

"Tell me, did you know Rav Kook, of blessed memory?"

"In fact, I did know the rabbi. I was privileged to hear his lofty Torah and inspiring discourses."

Abruptly, the old man burst into tears. "Oh, what a shame! What a terrible shame I failed to listen to him!" he sobbed.

After a few minutes, he regained his composure and told his story.

"In the early 1920s," the man began, "I was a successful industrialist in a large city in Poland. One day I decided to make a trip to *Eretz Yisrael* and spend the Passover holiday in Jerusalem. Being a religious Jew, I visited Rav Kook soon after arriving. He welcomed me warmly and encouraged me to seek out the good of the land and consider settling there.

"After a few weeks of touring, I returned to the Chief Rabbi and asked him what I should do regarding the second day of *Yom Tov*, seeing that I was a tourist.

"The Rav answered me with a smile. 'Decide now to bring your family here and build a factory in the Land. Then you can observe one day of *Yom Tov* already this Passover, like all residents of *Eretz Yisrael*.'

"I didn't think Rav Kook's response was a serious one. Since the holiday was still a few weeks away, I decided to return later on and pose the question again, when it would be more practical.

"A few days before Passover, I returned to Rav Kook and asked him once more.

"This time, the Rav's tone was stern. 'I already told you that you should move here. Then you may keep one day of *Yom Tov* starting now, even if you need to return to Poland after Passover to settle your affairs.'

"I said to him, 'I'm sorry, rabbi. I have given it much thought, but in the final analysis, *da'ati la-hazor* – my intention is to return to the Diaspora. How then can I celebrate like the residents of *Eretz Yisrael*?'

"The Rav banged on the table in anger. 'Your *da'at* is to return? Your intention to return? That is nothing but *lack* of *da'at* [sense]!'"

The old man looked down, finishing his story in a broken voice. "I did not listen to the Rav. I returned to Poland. I lost my wife, my children, and my grandchildren in the Holocaust. Here I am today, alone and desolate. I have returned to Warsaw with nothing, after years of wandering in Russia. And I hear Rav Kook's prophetic words, constantly ringing in my ears: 'That is nothing but lack of *da'at*!'"

THE JOY OF PURIM

The following description of Purim festivities in Rav Kook's home in Jerusalem, celebrated together with students from his yeshiva, took place in the 1930s, under the shadow of the rise of Nazi Germany.

Rav Kook, who had studied in the famed Volozhin yeshiva in his youth, transplanted the Volozhiner Purim merriment to his own yeshiva in Jerusalem, Mercaz HaRav.

Just as he would completely immerse himself in the special holiness of the Sabbath and holidays, so too, the joy of Purim would radiate from his entire being. On Purim, his happiness was evident in his exuberant speech; in his eyes, lit up like two merry torches; in the quickness of his movements; and in the lively content of his "Purim Torah."

The joy began on Purim evening. The yeshiva students hastened to the Rav's house wearing a riot of masks and costumes. Some were clothed in the long black coats worn by rabbis and rabbinical judges; others dressed in the shtreimels and colorful striped cloaks typical of the ultra-Orthodox of Jerusalem. A few arrived with exotic turbans and keffiyehs, while others wore the flat caps and short-sleeve shirts of manual laborers.

The Purim festivity was a mixed multitude of colors and hues, a cacophony of singing, cantorial renditions, Talmudic sing-song, and the melodious trope of Megillah reading. In addition to the yeshiva students, many prominent Jerusalemites showed up: Torah scholars and academics, political activists and writers, all of whom came to visit the Chief Rabbi in a time of exuberant happiness.

Rav Kook spoke of the *simhah* of the Jewish people, an inner joy that sings within the soul. This joy is not like the superficial delight of other nations, one that comes from transient pleasures and fades away in the blink of an eye. *"O Israel, do not rejoice in joy like the nations"* (Hosea 9:1). No, no, he emphasized. Our joy is fundamentally different.

Our custom is to wear costumes on Purim, the rabbi explained, because it is an auspicious time to frustrate the plans of the prosecuting angel. Temporarily, we adopt the customs of Amalek: we wear his clothes, become inebriated, and act frivolously. The prosecuting angel sees us as one of his own and forgets about us. In this way, the Sages' directive to drink on Purim enables us to abrogate the evil designs of Amalek.

In the middle of his speech, Rav Kook suddenly stood up and began to sing with great elation, *"Do not fear, My servant Jacob! Do not fear, do not fear!"* (Jeremiah 46:27) Then, to confuse the prosecuting angel, he sang the same tune, but translated the verse to Russian. In the following talks, he interjected Russian, German, and English words, thus adding to the general Purim spirit.

When the festivities reached their height, the Rav stood at the head of the table and began a lengthy Purim discourse. He examined every mitzvah in the Torah, interpreting each one as a source for the obligation to drink on Purim. With a wonderful blend of erudition and ingenuity, he derived from every mitzvah a metaphorical, homiletic, mystical, or even literal proof that one is obligated to drink "until one is unable to distinguish between cursed Haman and blessed Mordechai" (*Megillah* 7b).

Waging War on Amalek

That was the year in which persecution and violence burst forth across Germany. Synagogues were ransacked and set on fire; Jewish books were burned on public pyres; and Jews were beaten, robbed, and deported. Rav Kook sensed the impending Holocaust. Suddenly, he rose, slid his hat to the side of his head like a soldier, girded his belt, and barked out like a drill sergeant, "Come, my sons! Let us forge a battalion to wage war on Amalek!"

Everyone stood at attention, and the rabbi marched before them. Shouting commands in garbled Russian, he led his "battalion" through the corridors of the house. He sang, and they repeated after him, "Blot out! Blot out! Blot out the memory of Amalek!" He passed among the columns of "soldiers," singing with a military tune, *"Let the tribes of His nation sing His praise; for God will avenge His servants' blood, and bring vengeance upon His foes"* (Deuteronomy 32:43). The rabbi's eyes blazed, his body shook with emotion, and all marched after him in song.

Rav Kook then discharged the "troops" and they returned to the yeshiva, where he lectured on the special portion of the Jewish people.

> Our lot may be one of troubles, but nonetheless, *"Fortunate is the people for whom it is thus"* (Psalms 144:15). Even if we are persecuted all over the world, we are still privileged, since *"Fortunate is the people for whom the Eternal is their God"* (ibid).
>
> Israel never truly sins. Even in the time of Haman, they only bowed to the idols to show their allegiance; they did not really worship them. Sometimes a Jew puts on a costume and pretends to be a sinner. But on the inside, he is as pure as crystal.
>
> Amalek declared war on Israel. And precisely in times of war, we must engage in Torah study. In the terrifying abyss of the battle between purity and impurity, we make our home in the depths of Torah.

THE SHOFAR OF REDEMPTION

Zalman Shazar, the third president of the State of Israel, was a childhood friend of Rav Kook's most prominent disciple – Rabbi David Cohen, the Rav HaNazir. Shazar and Rabbi Cohen both relocated to Jerusalem, where they renewed their former friendship.

Zalman Shazar described an extraordinary encounter that he witnessed during the month of Elul, the month of reflection and repentance leading up to Rosh Hashanah.

When I rediscovered Rav David Cohen in Jerusalem, he was steadily ascending the world of mysticism and silence. One day in Elul, I went to visit him in Rav Kook's house. It was before the High Holidays, and I wanted to absorb some of his spirit of purity and holiness.

Upon arriving, I was informed that Rav David was in Rav Kook's study. The rabbis were reviewing the *kavanot,* the special Kabbalistic intentions for blowing the shofar on Rosh Hashanah.

I summoned the courage, and allowed myself to peek into the room. I froze at the sight, totally mesmerized.

The two scholars were both standing, eyes shut. Rav Kook called out the sounds – *tekiyah! shevarim-teruah! tekiyah!* – and Rav David blew the shofar.

But these were no ordinary shofar blasts. The blasts sounded as if they originated from another world. In those moments, I felt that I was hearing the shofar of our redemption. In my mind's eye, I saw the words of the daily prayer, *"Sound the great shofar for our freedom; lift up the banner to bring our exiles together."* This was the messianic shofar, announcing the ingathering of the exiles!

I was shaken to the very depths of my soul. That holy sight, and those inspiring sounds, will be forever engraved in my memory.

Rabbi David Cohen, the Rav HaNazir, and Rabbi Arieh Levin

STAY IN THE LAND!

One of the last people to speak with Rav Kook before his death was Prof. Hermann Zondek. Director of Jerusalem's Bikur Cholim hospital, Zondek treated the rabbi in a guest house in the Kiryat Moshe neighborhood of Jerusalem during his final illness. The doctor was amazed at the rabbi's concern and empathy for everyone with whom he came in contact – even during his last hours, when suffering intense pain.

Professor Zondek was an early victim of the rise of Nazism in Germany. In 1933, while treating patients in his Berlin hospital, he was called to his office. There, an SS officer informed Zondek that he was dismissed from his position as director of the Berlin City Hospital – effective immediately. His service during World War I as a military physician, his highly respected medical research, and his well-placed patients, which included German chancellors – all these counted for naught.

That very night, Zondek fled Germany. He later commented, "It was only after I left Germany that I realized that we, the Jews of Germany, had been living until 1933 in a fool's paradise."

Two years later, the doctor was working in Jerusalem, treating the aged Chief Rabbi in his final days. "A person's true nature is revealed during illness," he noted. "The Rav bore his terrible suffering with great wisdom."

In his final hour, Rav Kook was in severe pain. The room was full of people, and his colleague-disciple Rabbi Yaakov Moshe Charlap sat by his bed.

"About half an hour before his death," Zondek recalled, "the Rav took my hand in his. His voice thick with emotion, he told me, 'I hope that the prominent sons of our people will not leave our land, but will remain here to help build it up.' And then he pleaded, 'Please, stay here in the Land of Israel!'

"The truth is that this incident took place not long after I had come to the country. I had many difficulties adjusting. Much of what I found was not to my liking, and I was seriously considering leaving. But the Rav's heartfelt appeal, at that critical juncture, was a decisive factor in my decision to stay in our land. As a result, I put down roots here."

Jaffa Road, Jerusalem's main thoroughfare, packed with mourners during Rav Kook's funeral procession (Wikimedia Commons)

FINAL REQUESTS

It was the first of Elul when the Rav HaNazir arrived at the guest house where Rav Kook was staying in Kiryat Moshe. Exactly twenty years had passed since that first transformative encounter in Switzerland. This time he held in his hands a special document to show his dying master.

For twelve years, the Rav HaNazir had labored to organize Rav Kook's writings into a systematic, comprehensive work. As his revered master lay on his death bed, he showed him the beginning fruits of his labor – the title page of the first volume of *Orot HaKodesh*. Rav Kook rejoiced; and he shed tears.

On the day of his death, Rav Kook motioned to his son, Rav Tzvi Yehudah, to come close. "Please pay off any outstanding debts. I do not want to owe anyone, not even the smallest amount." He then made a second request: "Please prepare my writings for publication. However, take care that the only title given to me is 'rabbi.'"

With great effort, Rav Kook turned his face towards the scholars in the room. When it became clear that his soul would soon depart, the people cried out, "*Shema Yisrael!*" Rav Kook whispered after them, "*Shema Yisrael,*" breathing his final breath with the word *echad* – one. "*The Eternal is one.*"

"When the Rav passed away," the Rav HaNazir wrote, "we heard a heavenly voice. The voice called out, '*Haim, ad olam!*' 'Life, forever!' Even after completing life in this world, the soul continues, and it grows even stronger, with blessing, in eternal life."

USSISHKIN'S EULOGY

During a session of the 19ᵗʰ Zionist Congress in Switzerland, the delegates received the bitter news: Rabbi Abraham Isaac HaKohen Kook, the Chief Rabbi of Eretz Yisrael, had passed away earlier that evening in Jerusalem. Overcome by grief and mourning, the session was brought to an early close.

When the assembly reopened, Dr. Chaim Weizmann invited Menachem Ussishkin, respected Zionist leader and president of the JNF, to say a few words in honor of the beloved Chief Rabbi. The text below is from Ussishkin's eulogy at the Congress.

World Zionist Organization leaders on their arrival in New York, 1921. From left: Albert Einstein, Chaim Weizmann, Menachem Ussishkin (Wikimedia Commons)

Today, the Jewish nation is cloaked in deep mourning. One of the preeminent scholars of our generation has departed.

But I will not speak about his greatness in Torah. The speaker after me, Rabbi Meir Berlin, will speak of this. I will speak, not of the *Gaon*, the brilliant scholar, Rav Kook; but of the *man*, Rav Kook....

The first time I heard his name was from that unique luminary of our generation, Hayim Bialik.[16] After Bialik's first visit in *Eretz Yisrael*, he gave me a report of everything he saw. But his greatest enthusiasm

---

[16] Hayim Nahman Bialik (1873-1934), a pioneer of modern Hebrew poetry, widely regarded as Israel's national poet. Like Rav Kook, he studied in the famed Volozhin yeshiva in his youth.

concerned a certain Jew whom he had met, then rabbi of the small town of Jaffa. He told me wonders about this man's wisdom, his Torah and breadth of knowledge, and his tremendous expertise – not only in Torah, but also in the latest philosophies. And over all of this, Bialik added, hovers a towering personality in its depth, love, and dedication, and in its approach toward the new phenomena in the world.

When I made my second trip to *Eretz Yisrael*, I knew that I must meet this man whose fame precedes him. When I met him, I recognized that Bialik's description was accurate. Rav Kook was flowing with ideas – brilliant, sparkling ideas, regarding all aspects of life. When you spoke with him – or more precisely, when he spoke, for it was impossible to have a conversation with him, he would always lead the conversation, while others would listen and absorb – you would be exposed to such a wealth of ideas and views that sometimes you had to struggle to fully grasp their depth. You could not help but be enthralled with the brilliance of his ideas and the beauty of his imagery. After conversing with him, you always left the room with some new view, some new concept, or some new insight, regardless of whether you agreed with him.

Even though his views on life, and especially regarding our national life in Israel, were original and dazzling, Rav Kook remained with both feet firmly entrenched in our ancient traditions. He did not move a hair's breadth from the tenets of our fathers and ancestors. Yet he possessed a radically different approach on how to bring understanding of this tradition to the new and changing world that confronts us.

First of all, there must be a profound soul-connection between the old and new generations. His admiration for youth in general, and particularly the youth living in *Eretz Yisrael* – youth thousands of miles away from his own worldview – was like a father's understanding of his son, a father who wishes to instruct his son and draw him close with insight and love.

Many of you have heard his remarkable reply to a prominent scholar, a rabbi who criticized him for his cordial relations with the anti-religious youth. "How can you join forces with these people in common causes?"

The Rav responded by noting that the Holy Temple had separate courtyards. Some areas were only for priests; others were for Levites, or regular Israelites, or women. And there was one special place called the *Kodesh HaKodashim*, the Holy of Holies. There, only the High Priest was allowed to enter, and only once a year, on the holiest day of the year.

All this was true when the Temple was standing. Then there were separate areas for each sector of the nation, and each person knew where he was allowed and where he was not allowed to enter.

"However," Rav Kook said, "what do you think it was like while they were *constructing* the Temple? Then there were certainly no barriers. The workers went to any area that required their skills. Even into the Holy of Holies."[17]

Nowadays, the Rav concluded, we are building "the Third Temple." We are in the process of building. There are no – and there must not be any – barriers between the young generation and us, between the religious and the secular. We are all busy with one project; we are all working toward one goal. First, let us build this Temple. Afterwards we may discuss our differences....

That was Rav Kook's philosophy, from the first day that he arrived in the country, until his final day.

---

[17] As the Talmud teaches in tractate *Me'ilah* 14a: "First they would build, and only afterward would they sanctify the area."

Rabbi Tzvi Yehudah Kook

Jerusalem

Rabbi Tzvi Yehudah HaKohen Kook (1891-1982)
Oil painting by Tamar Rimon (1990)

Timeline	for Rabbi Tzvi Yehudah HaKohen Kook
1891	Born Passover eve in Zeimel, Lithuania, where his father served as rabbi.
1904	Arrived in *Eretz Yisrael*, after his father's appointment as Chief Rabbi of Jaffa (age 13).
1906	Studied in the Torat Chaim yeshiva in the Old City of Jerusalem (age 15).
1909	Began arranging and publishing his father's writings, including *Shabbat Ha'Aretz*, dealing with the laws of the Sabbatical Year (age 18).
1914-1919	Stranded with his father in Switzerland during WWI, they utilized the time for intensive Torah study ("We learned the entire Torah twice," he later said) (age 23-28).
1920	Returned together with his father to Jerusalem (age 29).
1924	Worked as director of his father's yeshiva, Mercaz HaRav, and lectured there (age 32).
1935	After his father's passing, he spent the next 15 years in intensive labor to arrange and publish his father's writings, starting with his Halakhic works (age 44).
1952	Appointed dean of Mercaz HaRav after Rabbi Yaakov Moshe Charlap's demise (age 61).
1982	Passed away in Jerusalem on Purim. Buried next to his father in Jerusalem's ancient Mount of Olives cemetery (age 90).

REJECTING THE LAND OF ISRAEL

A dispirited discussion took place at Beit HaRav, Rav Kook's house in Jerusalem, not long after the end of World War II. The Chief Rabbi had passed away ten years earlier; now it was his son, Rabbi Tzvi Yehudah Kook, who sat at the head of the table.

One participant at the Sabbath table had brought up a disturbing topic: the phenomenon of visitors touring *Eretz Yisrael* and then criticizing the country after returning to their homes. "These visitors complain about everything: the heat, the poverty, the backwardness, the political situation – and discourage other Jews from moving here," he lamented.

Rav Tzvi Yehudah responded by telling over the following parable, one he had heard in the name of Rabbi Samuel Mohilever.[18]

> There was once a wealthy man who sought the hand of a certain young lady. She was the most beautiful girl in town, and was blessed with many talents and a truly refined character. Her family was not well-off, so they were eager about a possible match with the prosperous fellow.
>
> The young woman, however, was not interested in the match. Rich or not, the prospective suitor was

---

[18] Rabbi Samuel Mohilever (1824-1898), the rabbi of Białystok in Poland, was a pioneer of Religious Zionism and a founder of the Hovevei Zion movement.

known to be coarse and ill-mannered. She refused to meet with him.

The father asked her to at least meet with the young man in their home, so as not to embarrass him. "After all, one meeting doesn't obligate you to marry him!" To please her father, the young woman agreed.

The following Sabbath afternoon, the fellow arrived at the house as arranged, and was warmly received by the father. Shortly afterwards, his daughter made her entrance. But her hair was uncombed, and she wore a faded, crumpled dress and shabby house slippers. Appalled at her disheveled appearance, it did not take long before the young man excused himself and made a hurried exit.

"What everyone says about this girl — it's not true," exclaimed the astonished young man to his friends. "She's hideous!"

Rav Tzvi Yehudah stopped briefly, surveying the guests seated around the table. "Superficially, it would appear that the brash young fellow had rejected the young woman. But in fact, it was *she* who had rejected him."

"The same is true regarding the Land of Israel," the rabbi explained. "*Eretz Yisrael* is a special land, only ready to accept those who are receptive to its unique spiritual qualities. The Land does not reveal its inner beauty to all who visit. Not everyone is worthy to perceive its special holiness."

"It may appear as if the dissatisfied visitors are the ones who reject the Land of Israel," he concluded. "But in fact, it is the Land that rejects them!"

A thoughtful silence pervaded the room. Those present were stunned by the parable and the rabbi's impassioned delivery. Then one of the guests observed, "Reb Tzvi Yehudah, your words are suitable for a son of your eminent father, may his memory be a blessing!"

Rav Tzvi Yehudah's response was indeed appropriate for Rav Kook's son. When visitors from outside the country would approach the Chief Rabbi for a blessing, Rav Kook would quote from the Book of Psalms, "*May God bless you from Zion*" (128:5).

Then he would ask: What exactly is this "blessing from Zion"? In fact, the content of the blessing is described in the continuation of the verse: "*May you see the goodness of Jerusalem.*"

The rabbi would explain: "The verse does not say that one should merit seeing Jerusalem; but that one should merit seeing 'the *goodness* of Jerusalem.' Many people visit Jerusalem. But how many of them merit seeing the inner goodness hidden in the holy city?"

"And *that*," he concluded, "is God's special blessing from Zion."

"Beit HaRav" – Rav Kook's home and yeshiva in Jerusalem

DRAFTING YESHIVA STUDENTS

Rabbi She'ar Yashuv Cohen, Chief Rabbi of Haifa and son of the Rav HaNazir, told the story of his part in defending Jerusalem during the 1948 War of Independence:

During the winter of 5708 [1947-1948], I was one of the younger students at the Mercaz HaRav yeshiva. I was also a member of the Haganah, the pre-state Jewish defense organization. This was during the period of Arab rioting and attacks that erupted following the United Nations' vote on the 29th of November, 1947, to establish a Jewish state.

In those days, there was much discussion in Mercaz HaRav whether the yeshiva students should enlist to fight and defend. Both my father, the Rav HaNazir, and Rav Tzvi Yehudah were of the opinion that everyone was obligated to go out and fight. This was a *milhemet mitzvah*, a compulsory war in which all are expected to participate.

However, those close to the head of the yeshiva, Rabbi Yaakov Moshe Charlap, argued that yeshiva students should continue their Torah studies in the yeshiva, and the merit of their Torah learning would bring victory in battle. They would quote the verse in Isaiah 62:6, "*On your walls, Jerusalem, I have posted watchmen,*" explaining that these watchmen protecting the city are in fact scholars, diligent in their Torah study.

At that time, the situation in the Jewish Quarter in Jerusalem's Old City was desperate. I came up with the idea of organizing a group of yeshiva students to establish a "Fighting-Defense Yeshiva" in the Jewish Quarter. The yeshiva's daily schedule would be comprised of eight hours for defense and guard duty, eight hours for Torah study, and eight hours for rest and sleep.[19]

The proposal was brought before the Haganah command and was approved. But those close to Rabbi Charlap were vehemently opposed to the idea. The controversy within Mercaz HaRav disturbed me deeply and caused me great anguish.

One day, as I exited the yeshiva, I saw huge notices posted at the entrance to the yeshiva. It was a broadside quoting Rav Abraham Isaac Kook, of blessed memory, that yeshiva students should not be drafted into the army. When I read the notices, I was in shock. Was I acting against the teachings of our master, Rav Kook?

Agitated and upset, I made my way down the road toward Jerusalem's Zion Square. There I saw a figure walking toward me, slightly limping. As he came closer, I saw that it was Rav Tzvi Yehudah. I felt very close to Rav Tzvi Yehudah; he was like an uncle to me.

When he saw my shocked face, Rav Tzvi Yehudah became concerned. "What happened, She'ar Yashuv? Why do you look like that? Don't be afraid. Tell me!"

Under the pressure of his questioning, I told him about my efforts to organize a "fighting yeshiva" in the Jewish Quarter, and my distress when I saw the posters which indicated that we were acting against his father's guidance.

When he heard my words, Rav Tzvi Yehudah was horrified. He grabbed me by my shoulders and roared, "This is a complete forgery! A distortion and utter falsehood!" He was so upset, his shouts echoed down the street.

After calming down, he explained that the notices had quoted a letter his father had written in London during the First World War.

---

[19] Rabbi She'ar Yashuv Cohen's "Fighting-Defense Yeshiva" was a precursor to the Hesder Yeshiva program, which alternates army service and yeshiva studies in a five-year program. The first Hesder Yeshiva was established in the Kerem BeYavneh yeshiva in 1953.

The letter dealt with drafting yeshiva students who had escaped from Russia to England. Rav Kook felt that these students should be exempt from the draft, just as the British exempted other clergy students.

But *here* – Rav Tzvi Yehudah motioned emphatically with his hands – *here* we are fighting for our hold on the Land of Israel and the holy city of Jerusalem. This is undoubtedly a *milhemet mitzvah*; whereas in England, the demand was that the yeshiva students fight for a foreign army.

The rabbi's words reassured me. I asked if he would be willing to write them down so that they could be publicized. He agreed. The rabbi publicized a broadside in which he objected to the use of his father's letter to Rabbi Hertz, Chief Rabbi of England, during World War I.

I also asked Rav Tzvi Yehudah to publish his views on the matter in a more detailed and reasoned format. He replied that there is no point in composing an article when the city is under siege and the printing presses are closed down. However, I was able to obtain a special permit from the Defense Board, so that a pamphlet containing five articles was published soon after.

In his article, Rav Tzvi Yehudah explained that joining the army at that time was important for three reasons:

1. To save lives (*pikuah nefesh*);
2. To fulfill the mitzvah of conquering and settling the Land of Israel (*mitzvat yishuv ha'aretz*);
3. Due to the great public *kiddush Hashem*, sanctification of God's Name, when the nation of Israel is redeemed from danger.

Even though I was the one who had initiated the pamphlet's publication, I did not receive a copy when it was printed. Due to special circumstances, several months passed before I received a copy.

I was one of the volunteers who succeeded in finding a way to slip inside the walls of the Old City. I joined the fighters there, and I was seriously wounded in battle.

When the Old City fell to the Arab Legion on May 27th, 1948, I was taken prisoner. The

The Arab Legion attacking the Jewish Quarter of Jerusalem, May 1948 (John Phillips for Life Magazine)

Jordanian commander was shocked to discover that only 26 of the surrendering Jewish soldiers survived the battles without serious injury. Embarrassed to return victorious to Jordan with such a small group of prisoners, he decided to also take wounded soldiers.

After seven months as a prisoner in Jordan, we were returned to Israel in a prisoner exchange deal. I was taken to Zichron Ya'akov to recuperate, and Rav Tzvi Yehudah came to visit me the first morning after my arrival.

The morning of Rav Tzvi Yehudah's visit, as I was removing my tefillin after morning prayers, I peered out the window and saw Rav Tzvi Yehudah slowly making his way up the mountain. Afterward, I found out that he had taken the very first bus from Jerusalem, and had traveled early in the morning all the way to Zichron Ya'akov in order to greet me.

I ran toward him, and he hugged and kissed me. He cried over me like a child. The truth is that my situation was so grave that my family and friends had nearly given up all hope. Until then, such a thing had never happened – returning alive from captivity in an Arab country. But the Jordanian King Abdullah had wanted to show the world that he was an enlightened monarch who respected international law....

After recovering from his outburst of emotion, Rav Tzvi Yehudah put his hand in his coat pocket and brought out a small pamphlet containing his article about defending the country. Inside was a personal inscription:

> For my dear beloved friend – the initiator, advisor, and solicitor [of this tract]. This pamphlet is set aside, from the day it was printed, until *"God's redeemed will return in peace, and joyfully come to Zion."*

Decades later, I still have that treasured pamphlet carefully stored in my possession.

Chief Rabbi Emeritus of Haifa, Rabbi Shear Yashuv Cohen, in his study. On the wall is a painting of his father, the Rav HaNazir (impromptu photograph by his wife, Rabbanit Dr. Naomi Cohen).

ISRAEL INDEPENDENCE DAY

May 14, 1948. A few hours before the Sabbath, on the fifth of Iyyar, the National Council assembled in Tel Aviv to announce the establishment of the State of Israel.

The decision to establish the state was not simple. It was obvious that following the announcement, the Arab armies would commence a joint attack on the fledgling state, whose army was still in the process of being organized, and armed with inadequate and outdated equipment. There was also a real concern that the nations of the world would not recognize the Jewish state, and the young country would remain isolated. Nevertheless, the country's leaders took courage and declared the establishment of the State of Israel.[20]

---

[20] The greatest miracle of the establishment of the State of Israel, Rav Tzvi Yehudah taught, was not the military victory of a fledgling state over the armies of five enemy countries. It was the remarkable courage to make that fateful decision and announce the establishment of an independent state.

Under intense pressure from the US State Department not to declare a state, as well as belligerent threats of the surrounding Arab countries that they would attack and destroy the Jewish community in *Eretz Yisrael*, this decision was not a trivial matter. The motion to declare a state only passed by a thin majority in David Ben-Gurion's cabinet.

One member of the cabinet, Moshe Sharett, recorded his emotions that day. "There was a sense of excitement together with a clear premonition of danger, such as one might feel while standing on a cliff, ready to leap into a yawning chasm. We felt as though we stood on a very high crest, where roaring winds were brewing about us, and that we had to stand fast."

For Rav Tzvi Yehudah, the founding of the State of Israel was a realization of the Biblical prophecies. Its establishment after two millennia of stateless wanderings and exile was a Divine miracle, a revelation of God's hand in all its glory. This historical event, he taught, was not just *reishit tzemihat ge'ulateinu*, the "beginning of the flowering of our redemption." This was a step in the process of redemption itself![21]

The establishment of governmental agencies and frameworks of self-rule, the extraordinary return of Jews from around the world, the remarkable advances in settling *Eretz Yisrael* and developing its agriculture and economy – Rav Tzvi Yehudah saw in all of these historic events a fulfillment of the prophecy of the End of Days. He would frequently quote Rabbi Abba's statement in *Sanhedrin* 98a regarding Ezekiel's prophetic vision:

> And you, O mountains of Israel, shoot forth your branches and yield your fruit to My people Israel, because they are about to come. (36:8)

Rabbi Abba commented: "There is no more manifest sign of the End of Days than this!" In other words, the agricultural flourishing of *Eretz Yisrael* is a sure indication of the final redemption of Israel.

Rav Tzvi Yehudah taught that Jewish autonomy is not merely a physical concept. Independence is a spiritual concept. The freedom of the Jewish people from foreign rule is not only a political matter; it is

---

This courageous decision, Rav Tzvi Yehudah wrote, was the true miracle of Yom HaAtzma'ut. The spirit of valor is a miracle from above, an inspired inner drive spurring one to rise to the pressing needs of the hour.

21 Rav Tzvi Yehudah's outlook follows Maimonides' opinion that the Messianic Era is not an era of supernatural miracles, and only differs from the present in Israel's independence "from the rule of foreign powers" (*Mishneh Torah*, Laws of Kings 12:2, based on the Talmudic dictum in *Berakhot* 34b).

also a religious value. He therefore perceived holiness in the State of Israel and the Israel Defense Force.

For the individual, he explained, there is an essential difference between the material and the spiritual. But for *Klal Yisrael*, for the entire people of Israel, these are spiritual matters. Military strength, economic prosperity, agricultural accomplishments – these are all part of the redemption process, because they relate, not to individuals, but to *Klal Yisrael* and its ability to accomplish its universal mission.

"Let Us Rejoice and Be Glad!"

Rav Tzvi Yehudah's students observed how their teacher's outlook was evident in his inspired elation when celebrating Yom HaAtzma'ut, Israel Independence Day.

One of his prominent disciples, Rabbi Chaim Drukman, dean of the Or Etzion yeshiva, described how the rabbi would rejoice.

> Because he saw the great value of the State of Israel, our rabbi was filled with tremendous joy on Yom HaAtzma'ut. Whoever has not seen him rejoicing on Yom HaAtzma'ut, never saw true joy in his life. Those who merited witnessing this joy, who heard him lecture on Yom HaAtzma'ut – they saw how he completely identified with the grandeur of the day, with its holiness and unique essence.
>
> During his talks on Yom HaAtzma'ut, the rabbi would display such an intensity of emotions that sometimes he was brought to tears. You could sense how his spirits sang, how his soul rejoiced in *"This is the day that God has made!"* (Psalms 118:24) Therefore, and due to our awareness of the greatness of the hour – *"Let us rejoice and be glad in it"* (ibid.).

Rabbi Zalman Melamed, rabbi of the town of Beit El and head of the yeshiva there, related:

> To watch Rav Tzvi Yehudah on Yom HaAtzma'ut was a unique experience. He was completely shining, exuding light and festivity. It was enough to see him, and you felt your spirits lift up. During the Yom HaAtzma'ut celebrations and prayers at the yeshiva, he prayed at length, with great exhilaration and depth, lifting up the entire congregation with him.

Rabbi Joseph Bramson, author and lecturer, recalled:

> His elation was so unique, his joy at this revelation of God's deliverance of Israel. When he sang and danced, it appeared as if he was walking on the ground and holding his students' hands like everyone else in the dance circle. But in fact, he was somewhere between heaven and earth. Every bone in his body sang out with pure gratitude to the Redeemer of Israel.

There are many who speak of the State of Israel and recognize its benefits and accomplishments. But they only see the external aspects. They have not yet perceived its inner content. Rav Tzvi Yehudah was one of the select few who grasped, in all its profound depth, the Divine event that took place when the State was established that Friday afternoon in 1948.

RETURNING TO THE KOTEL

In a sense, it all started in the fall of 1966. During the annual memorial for Rav Kook on the third of Elul, Rav Tzvi Yehudah surprised the people gathered at Beit HaRav with an unusual statement. "My father labored for the sake of the Jewish people when he was alive in this world," he said. "And he continues to work for the Jewish people, with even greater strength and merit, while in the next world."

These labors, Rav Tzvi Yehudah noted, are connected to the Jewish people's possession of *Eretz Yisrael*. Especially this year:

> As his stay in the next world lengthens, so his power and influence grow. Each year, he conquers an additional realm in the "yeshiva on high," and these conquests continue and spread.
>
> This year is the 31st year since his passing [in 1935]. The number of conquests is thus 31 – corresponding to the number of Canaanite kings that Joshua subdued [when conquering the Land of Israel]."

The following spring, the security situation in Israel deteriorated rapidly. Egypt expelled UN peacekeeping forces in the Sinai Peninsula and began massing troops on Israel's border. On May 22, Egypt blocked the Straits of Tiran, passageway for almost all of Israel's oil. The following week, Egypt and Jordan signed a defense pact, posing a further threat to the young country. (Syria had signed a mutual defense agreement the previous November.) And the Iraqi army deployed troops and armored units in Jordan.

In Israel, spirits were low and tensions high.

111

During Israel Independence Day celebrations at the Mercaz HaRav yeshiva, Rav Tzvi Yehudah usually spoke about the spiritual significance of the day. But this year, the nineteenth year of the State of Israel, his address took on a different tone. It was less lecture, more prophetic vision.

Rav Tzvi Yehudah recalled his visceral pain nineteen years previous, when the 1947 UN Partition Plan was approved, assigning parts of the Jewish homeland to an Arab state. People streamed into the streets to celebrate and rejoice. "But I could not go out and join in the celebration. I sat alone and silent; a heavy burden lay upon me. During those first hours, I could not resign myself to what had been done. I could not accept the fact that, indeed, *'They have divided My land'* (Joel 4:2)"

The rabbi then stunned the audience as he thundered, "And where is our Hebron? Are we forgetting this? Where is our Shechem, our Jericho? Have we forgotten them?"

Rabbi Hanan Porat, well-known author, educator, and member of Knesset, was one of the Mercaz HaRav students who fought in the battle for Jerusalem. "I was in the yeshiva during that Independence Day celebration," Rabbi Porat recalled. "Rav Tzvi Yehudah's roars still reverberate in my ears. If I think back to lectures or speeches which influenced me, without a doubt it was this address that had the greatest impact on me."

He added, "We felt that our rabbi was speaking with prophetic spirit, that 'the Shechinah was speaking though his mouth.' The very walls shook. People looked at one other in wonder."

Rabbi Yisrael Ariel, another student of Mercaz HaRav who participated in the liberation of Jerusalem, told his story, which began soon after that momentous address in the yeshiva.

> When they announced preparations [of the reserve army] before the Six-Day War, I was called up as a paratrooper. For three weeks, we waited in orchards

near the Lod airport, ready to parachute into the Sinai Desert.

During these weeks of waiting, many thoughts passed in my head. What was the meaning of this war? Ten years earlier, the Sinai War had been fought, at the price of many lives. And in the end, nothing had been gained from it. What was the point of another war and the further spilling of precious blood?

I wrote my questions in a letter to Rav Tzvi Yehudah and the Rav HaNazir. But before I had a chance to mail my letter, the war broke out. Our division, under the command of Motta Gur, was re-assigned to Jerusalem. With God's mercy, we had the privilege of liberating the Old City and the Temple Mount.

As we made our way to the Temple Mount, it was rumored that two elders from Jerusalem had arrived. I was overcome with powerful emotions and an unbelievable feeling of elation. I was sure that these two elders must be the Messiah and Elijah the prophet....

When I descended from the Temple Mount to the Kotel, I discovered that the two elders were none other than our master, Rav Tzvi Yehudah, and the Rav HaNazir. We hugged, we kissed, and our tears flowed without stop....

I realized then that I had received the answer to my questions – directly from Rav Tzvi Yehudah and the Rav HaNazir. We had merited seeing, with our own eyes, God's return to Zion!

Rabbi Hanan Porat related his memories from the war:

On the fourth day of the war, we fought at Ammunition Hill. From there we went up to Mount Scopus and the Agusta Victoria hospital. We started making our way toward the Temple Mount. Suddenly – I couldn't believe my eyes – an army jeep passed by us, carrying Rav Tzvi Yehudah and the Rav HaNazir! They were wearing steel helmets, and the Rav HaNazir's long hair streamed out in the wind....

It was an otherworldly sight. The fact that these two holy scholars were among the first ones to reach the Kotel added another level of holiness to our return to the Kotel.

Rabbi Porat recalled how Rav Tzvi Yehudah cleaved to the stones of the Kotel. He prayed with intense fervor; and afterward he turned to the soldiers and kissed them. The Rav HaNazir, on the other hand, cleaved to the Kotel and never let go. He was soaring in elevated realms. This was typical of these two great figures; each one expressed himself in his own individual spiritual path.

The next day, several of Rav Tzvi Yehudah's students went to visit their master. They found Rav Tzvi Yehudah visiting the Rav HaNazir in his Jerusalem apartment. The two scholars were discussing the momentous events of the previous day.

IDF jeeps in Jerusalem after the Six-Day War (PikiWiki)

"Around eleven o'clock in the morning," Rav Tzvi Yehudah told the students, "an army officer knocked on my door. He told me that Rabbi Goren, the IDF Chief Rabbi, had invited me to come immediately to the Kotel. A jeep waited for me in the street."

The rabbi entered the vehicle, where he was joined by the Rav HaNazir (who was the father-in-law of Rabbi Goren). On the way to the Kotel, the officer told them the following story:

When the paratroopers arrived at the Kotel, one of the soldiers – a student at Mercaz HaRav – climbed up to the highest row of stones and waved the flag of Israel. Down below, the paratroopers shouted and cheered. The commander announced that the soldier deserved a prize for his action, and asked him what he wanted.

In the silence that followed, the soldier thought for a moment and replied, "The greatest prize for me would be to bring Rav Tzvi Yehudah Kook, the head of the Mercaz HaRav yeshiva, so that he will join us in our great joy."

The Rav HaNazir then startled those present with his account of the visit. "As we approached the Kotel, I saw Rav Kook, of blessed memory, standing there, wearing his Sabbath clothes." Surprised by the looks of confusion on the students' faces, he said, "But of course the Rav had to be there on that special day!

The Rav HaNazir and Rav Tzvi Yehudah at the Kotel, shortly after its liberation. On the left: Rabbi Yisrael Ariel.

THE GRAPE HARVEST

Yosef Kfir was embarrassed to be returning to yeshiva so late, but he had little choice. His parents owned and cultivated a vineyard in Kfar Pines, a religious *moshav* in northern Israel. Unfortunately, the family was still busy with the autumn grape harvest when the first day of Elul – the start of academic year in yeshivot – arrived. Yosef's father requested that he postpone leaving home until the harvest was finished. Two weeks passed before Yosef was able to return to his studies at Mercaz HaRav in Jerusalem.

On his first day back, the young man attended a lecture of the Rosh Yeshiva, Rabbi Tzvi Yehudah Kook. He had hoped that the rabbi would turn a blind eye to his absence, but that was not to be. As the students sat down around the table, Rav Tzvi Yehudah greeted Yosef and inquired why he was late in returning to the yeshiva. Eyes lowered, Yosef explained that his parents had required his help with the grape harvest. Understood, if not articulated, was the assumption that the rabbi would recognize the importance of honoring parents, even at the expense of his Torah studies.

Watching this brief exchange, the yeshiva students were surprised to see Rav Tzvi Yehudah jump up and turn to one of the bookshelves. The rabbi quickly located and pulled down a commentary on the Talmud by the renowned Hatam Sofer.[22]

The commentary analyzed a Talmudic debate between Rabbi Shimon and Rabbi Ishmael in *Berakhot* 35b. Rabbi Shimon taught that one should study Torah throughout the day, as indicated by a literal

---

[22] Rabbi Moses Sofer (1762-1839), rabbi of Pressburg (Bratislava) and leading Halakhic authority. He is commonly referred to by the name of his most popular work, a collection of Halakhic decisions entitled *Hatam Sofer*.

understanding of the verse, *"You shall meditate in the [words of Torah] day and night"* (Joshua 1:8). Rabbi Ishmael, however, disagreed. He ruled that one should combine the study of Torah with a worldly occupation.

Rav Tzvi Yehudah opened the commentary of the Hatam Sofer and read the text out loud, his voice betraying his excitement:

> In my humble opinion, Rabbi Ishmael only asserted that one should follow what it says, *"You shall harvest your grain, your wine and your oil"* (Deuteronomy 11:14), [even though this will impinge upon time available for Torah study] for those residing in the Land of Israel, at a time when the majority of the Jewish people dwell there. The reason being that, in this case, working the land and producing its holy fruit is itself a mitzvah – the mitzvah of *yishuv Eretz Yisrael*, settling the Land of Israel. It was in this context that the Torah commanded us, *"You shall harvest your grain."*
>
> Thus Boaz [of the Book of Ruth, a leading Torah scholar of his generation], winnowed barley in the threshing floor at night in order to fulfill this mitzvah.
>
> Just as one would not say, "I will not wear tefillin because I am currently busy studying Torah," so too, one cannot say, "I will not harvest my crops because I am busy studying Torah." (*Hiddushei Hatam Sofer* on *Sukkah* 36a)

His face shining, Rav Tzvi Yehudah explained the Hatam Sofer's viewpoint. It is inconceivable that one would decide not to wear tefillin because it takes away time from Torah study. So too, harvesting the produce of *Eretz Yisrael* is a mitzvah. When it is time to harvest, this takes precedence over Torah study!

117

With his impassioned words, the rabbi relieved Yosef's uneasiness, raising his spirits. After all, he had been occupied in fulfilling the mitzvah of settling the Land!

Yosef later observed: "On that day I gained a clearer grasp of the connection between my theoretical studies of Torah 'in the books,' and our practical, day-to-day life in *Eretz Yisrael*."

Decades later, Yosef's father became seriously ill. Yosef spent many nights at his father's bedside. A few days before his death, his father called out in the middle of the night. What was so vital that he needed to wake up his son at that hour?

His voice weak and unsteady, the old man whispered, "Do you remember what Rav Tzvi Yehudah said that day? How he spoke about the holy mitzvah of settling the Land of Israel and harvesting its fruits?"

Yosef's father was a true pioneer. He fully identified with the "Torah and Avodah" movement, combining the ideals of religious commitment and working the Land of Israel. Up to his final days, Rav Tzvi Yehudah's words served as the philosophical foundation and the Halakhic basis for his life's work.

Grape harvest (Givat Ada Archives/PikiWiki)

VISITING THE SICK

Rabbi Dr. Michael Zvi Nehorai, a professor at Bar Ilan University, recounted the following lesson he learned about how to visit the sick:

When Rav Tzvi Yehudah was hospitalized in Jerusalem's Sha'arei Tzedek hospital, suffering from intense pain in his legs, I went to visit him.

In great pain, the rabbi was moaning. As a student who felt very close to him, it was difficult for me to witness his distress. When I saw his state and heard his groans, I groaned too.

A month after Rav Tzvi Yehudah was released from the hospital and returned to teach at the yeshiva, the rabbi approached me.

"Don't you think it is time you learned the laws of *bikur holim*, the proper way to visit the sick?"

I had no idea what the rabbi was talking about.

Then he explained, "When visiting the sick, one should be upbeat and cheer them up. One shouldn't groan, 'Oy, oy....'"

"You are probably wondering," the rabbi continued, "why I didn't mention this to you right away. At the time, I was disturbed by your conduct, and I didn't want to reprimand you while I was still upset."

Rav Kook offered similar guidance about how one should visit the sick. During his final illness, he urged those who came to visit him to perform the mitzvah of *bikur holim* with *simhah*, with joy. He quoted a letter of Maimonides, who explained that the primary goal of this mitzvah is to encourage the sick so that they will not despair and give up hope. Therefore it is clear that visitors should display a cheerful and optimistic attitude.

Additionally, Rav Kook noted, visiting the sick is a mitzvah. It should be performed with joy, like any other mitzvah in the Torah.

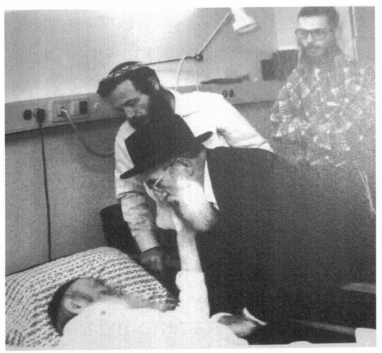

Chief Rabbi Shlomo Goren and Rabbi Chaim Drukman visiting Rav Tzvi Yehudah Kook in the hospital.

THE MERIT OF A DANCE

Rabbi Yisrael Ariel, who served as Chief Rabbi of Yamit and founded the Temple Institute in Jerusalem, related this story from 1973, when he was a student at Mercaz HaRav and was called up to fight in the Yom Kippur War.

During the Yom Kippur War, the army called up reserve soldiers to defend the country against the surprise Arab attack. Heavy fighting continued in the Golan Heights and the Sinai Desert for several weeks, through the holiday of Succoth.

Immediately following Succoth is a holiday of exuberant joy – Simhat Torah, when it is customary to celebrate the completion of reading the Torah with singing and dancing. During the war, however, many felt that it was improper to rejoice while the soldiers were fighting on the battlefield. Some of the yeshiva students also felt that public displays of joy were inappropriate.

But Rav Tzvi Yehudah was adamant: "We will teach the people to rejoice!" The rabbi, accompanied by a small band of students, danced on Simhat Torah morning in the streets of Jerusalem, as they made their way to the home of the Chief Rabbi. A few of the synagogue members also joined the yeshiva students, including my father.

When they reached King George Street, a passerby began to shout at them. "How dare you dance?" The man pointed an accusatory finger at the group. "The whole country is fighting for its life in this war, and you dance? Have you no shame?!"

Rav Tzvi Yehudah stopped and turned to him. "Why are you upset? Look at this Jew who is dancing with me" – and here he indicated my father. "His four sons are all currently fighting at various fronts. And

121

yet he dances and rejoices in the *simhah* of the Torah. You should also come and dance with us!"

At the very time that my father was dancing with Rav Tzvi Yehudah in Jerusalem, I was stationed on Mount Hermon in the Golan Heights with my brother Rabbi Yaakov Ariel [now Chief Rabbi of the city of Ramat Gan]. We were in grave danger, sprawled out on the ground while enemy shells whistled above us, exploding to our right and to our left.

Who knows? Perhaps it was the merit of that holy dance in honor of the Torah that saved our lives....

Chief Rabbis of Lod dancing with Sefer Torah, c. 1955 (PikiWiki)

"WHERE IS THE AGREEMENT?"

Rabbi Yehoshua Ben-Meir, founder and head of Shvut Rachel yeshiva, related his experiences as a young chaplain in the Israeli army, responsible for the identification and burial of casualties in the Yom Kippur War.

During the Yom Kippur War, I served as an army chaplain in an IDF division in the Golan Heights. It was a terrible war. The battles and the conditions were extraordinarily difficult. Every day we witnessed death up close.

We had been taught in the Mercaz HaRav yeshiva

Wreckage of Israeli M60 tank (Wikimedia Commons)

that the redemption of Israel is a process, one that grows and advances, progressing from strength to strength. But in this war, we experienced a sense of retreat. The blow was terrible, the pain was searing. In those trying times, I felt a tremendous need to examine and clarify my beliefs. I needed to understand how this bitterly fought war fit in the process of Israel's redemption.

After two months of fighting at the front, with no showers, in extremely harsh conditions, I received a short leave.

I travelled straight to Jerusalem. The hour was late – two o'clock in the morning. But I urgently needed to speak with the Rosh Yeshiva, Rav Tzvi Yehudah. I decided that I would first go to his house. Hesitantly, I knocked on the door of his modest apartment on Ovadiah Street.

The rabbi peeked through the peephole and immediately opened the door.

"Give me the document," he said.

Apparently the rabbi was expecting some document from the army. I was so grimy and dirty, I figured he failed to recognize me.

"Rabbi – it's me, Yehoshua Ben-Meir."

"Yes, yes," Rav Tzvi Yehudah responded. "Bring the document."

I had no idea what the rabbi was talking about.

He took my hand, led me into his room, and sat me down on a chair. Again he insisted, "Show me the paper."

"Rabbi, it's me, Yehoshua Ben-Meir from the yeshiva."

"Yes, I know. The document. Bring me the document."

I was completely baffled. I still figured that the rabbi did not recognize me because of all the grease and dirt.

"Rabbi, what document are you talking about?"

"You have an agreement with God how the redemption of Israel is supposed to take place. And God changed the agreement. So show me the document. Let us examine what is written there, and we will decide."

I heard the rabbi's words, and – for the first time since the war broke out – I suddenly began to cry. Tears rolled down my face, releasing the pain and bitterness bottled inside, softening the grief and misery from the horrible events that I had witnessed.

I was amazed how quickly the rabbi had understood me. In those few seconds, from when he saw me through the peephole until I entered the room, he had identified my problem and known the solution.

The rabbi sat with me for a long time, maybe two hours. He took down books from the shelves. Before starting to study a text, he said, "Perhaps you have not learned this. And if you have, perhaps you did not review it. And if you reviewed, perhaps you forgot. Did we not learn...?"

The first book he opened was the commentary of 13th-century scholar Rabbeinu Behaye. God sent Moses to Egypt to redeem the Israelites, but, at first, matters only got worse. Pharaoh instituted even harsher decrees against the Hebrew slaves. And Moses complained to God, *"Why have You made it worse for Your people? Why did you send me?"* (Exodus 5:22)

Commenting on this verse, Rabbeinu Behaye noted that this phenomenon is not unique to the redemption from Egypt. The future redemption will also be accompanied by many difficulties, by times of darkness that will conceal the light of redemption.

The rabbi continued to open other classical texts – books of the Maharal of Prague, the *Kuzari,* the Midrash – reviewing with me various sources. After two hours of study together, I left his small apartment feeling renewed and fortified. I was armed with the spiritual strength I needed to continue.

Rav Tzvi Yehudah had the genius to sense the needs of each student. He could plumb the depths of your soul and provide the exact response you needed.

References

Chapter 1 (Rav Kook Arrives in Jaffa): *Encyclopaedia of Religious Zionism*, vol. V, pp. 110-111.

Chapter 2 (The Blessing of a Kohen): *Hayei HaRe'iyah*, pp. 332-337; *Shivhei HaRe'iyah*, pp. 91-95; *Mo'adei HaRe'iyah*, pp. 529-532; *Sihot HaRe'iyah*, p. 209.

Chapter 3 (The Hetter Mekhirah for the Sabbatical Year): *Igrot HaRe'iyah*, vol. I.

Chapter 4 (The Visit to Merhavya): *Megged Yerahim*, vol. 174; *Eileh Massei*.

Chapter 5 (Dances of Teshuvah in Poriah): *Megged Yerahim*, vol. 156; *Encyclopedia of Founders and Builders of Israel*.

Chapter 6 (The Nazir of Jerusalem): *Malachim Kivnei Adam*, pp. 74-76.

Chapter 7: (The London Bomb Shelter): *Shivhei HaRe'iyah*, pp. 129-130.

Chapter 8 (The Balfour Declaration): *Mo'adei HaRe'iyah*, pp. 391-393; *Celebration of the Soul*, pp. 186-189; *Encyclopedia of Religious Zionism*, vol. 5, pp. 179-190; *Igrot HaRe'iyah* vol. III, pp. 100, 107-114.

Chapter 9 ("Who Are You, Great Mountain?"): *Mo'adei HaRe'iyah*, p. 403.

Chapter 10 (Planting a Tree in Magdiel): *Zehav Ha'Aretz* by Rabbi Ze'ev Gold (1982); *Mo'adei HaRe'iyah*, pp. 222-223.

Chapter 11 (Blasts That Penetrate the Heart): *Mo'adei HaRe'iyah*, pp. 65-66.

Bibliography

An Angel Among Men – *Impressions From the Life of Rav Avraham Yitzchak Hakohen Kook*, by Simcha Raz. Translated by Rabbi Moshe D. Lichtman. Published 2003.

Celebration of the Soul – *The Holidays in the Life and Thought of Rabbi Avraham Yitzchak Kook*. Translated by Rabbi Pesach Jaffe. Published by Genesis Jerusalem Press, 1992.

Hayei HaRe'iyah, by Rabbi Moshe Tzvi Neriah. Published 1983.

Malachim Knei Adam, by Simcha Raz. Published by Kol Mevaser, 1993.

Mashmia Yeshu'ah, by Simcha Raz, Hilah Volbershtin, and Rabbi Shalom Klein. Published by Or Etzion Publications, Mercaz Shapiro, 2009.

Megged Yerahim, a monthly journal produced by the Beit HaRav Kook Museum and Archival Center.

Mo'adei HaRe'iyah by Rabbi Moshe Tzvi Neriah. Published by Moriah, Jerusalem, 1982.

Shivhei HaRe'iyah, by Prof. Chaim Lifshitz. Published by Machon Harry Fischel, 1978.

Zichron Re'iyah, collection of articles edited by Isaac Raphael. Published by Mossad HaRav Kook, Jerusalem, 1986.

Rabbi Chanan Morrison

Rabbi Morrison grew up in Pennsylvania and graduated with a B.A. in Mathematics from Yeshiva University (New York). Pursuing advanced Talmudic studies in Jerusalem, he spent the next seven years studying in Jerusalem yeshivot, including the famed Yeshivat Mercaz HaRav, founded by Rabbi Abraham Isaac Kook in 1924. He taught Jewish studies for several years in Harrisburg, PA, before returning to Israel, settling down in a small community in the Judean Desert.

Rabbi Morrison is frequently featured on the Torah section of the Israel National News website, and his work can be read on his own website at http://ravkooktorah.org. He has published three books on Rav Kook's writings: *Gold from the Land of Israel* (Urim, 2006), *Silver from the Land of Israel* (Urim, 2010), and *Sapphire from the Land of Israel* (CreateSpace, 2013).

Praise for *Gold from the Land of Israel*

In these succinct and clearly written essays, Rabbi Morrison has succeeded in expounding on major themes from Rav Kook's thought. Those who are not familiar with the Rav's teachings will be exposed to the profound ideas and remarkable scope of his writings.
–Rabbi Yehoshua Magnes, Rosh Yeshiva at Mercaz HaRav

Rabbi Morrison has done a remarkable job presenting Rav Kook's teachings in a clear, approachable fashion. I highly recommend this book for anyone seeking a good introduction to the inspiring wisdom of this preeminent scholar.
–Rabbi David Samson

131

Made in the USA
Lexington, KY
26 April 2015